PSYCHOLOGY OF DIGITAL PERSUASION

How Technology Shapes Decisions

Diego Rodrigues

PERSUASIVETECH
PSYCHOLOGY OF DIGITAL PERSUASION
How Technology Shapes Decisions

2025 Edition
Author: Diego Rodrigues

Published by StudioD21.

CONTENTS

GREETINGS

Dear reader!

It is with great enthusiasm that I invite you to explore the fascinating mechanisms that shape our decisions in the digital environment. Choosing to delve into this topic demonstrates your desire to understand how modern technology uses psychology to influence our daily choices, emotions and behaviors.

In this book, **"PSYCHOLOGY OF DIGITAL PERSUASION: How Technology Shapes Decisions"**, we go far beyond the simple analysis of digital tools. Our goal is to reveal **the fundamental psychological principles** that underpin digital influence, from the emotional triggers used in persuasive interfaces to the algorithms that personalize our online experience in an almost imperceptible way.

We live in an era where notifications, recommendations and visual stimuli compete for our attention every second. Social networks, e-commerce platforms, streaming services and even productivity apps are designed to capture and maintain our engagement. But **What psychological strategies are behind this?** How does our mind process these interactions and why do we make certain decisions without realizing we have been influenced?

Throughout this book, we will explore **the classic models of persuasion**, the impacts of **artificial intelligence in human behavior**, the **role of the attention economy**, the risks of **excessive customization** and how the **neuroscience has been applied in digital marketing**. Additionally, we will discuss ethical issues and strategies for **strengthen your autonomy in the face of these invisible influences**.

Whether you are a professional in the field, a student of human behavior or simply someone interested in better understanding the forces that shape your decisions in the digital world, this book will be an essential tool to broaden your perception and awareness on the topic.

Get ready for an eye-opening journey. By the end of reading, you will not only have a deep understanding of **how and why are we persuaded in the digital environment**, but you will also be better able to **make conscious and strategic decisions** in the face of the technologies that are part of our daily lives.

I wish you an thought-provoking and transformative read!

ABOUT THE AUTHOR

www.linkedin.com/in/diegoexpertai

Best-Selling Author, Diego Rodrigues is an International Consultant and Writer specializing in Market Intelligence, Technology and Innovation. With 42 international certifications from institutions such as IBM, Google, Microsoft, AWS, Cisco, and Boston University, Ec-Council, Palo Alto and META.

Rodrigues is an expert in Artificial Intelligence, Machine Learning, Data Science, Big Data, Blockchain, Connectivity Technologies, Ethical Hacking and Threat Intelligence.

Since 2003, Rodrigues has developed more than 200 projects for important brands in Brazil, USA and Mexico. In 2024, he consolidates himself as one of the largest new generation authors of technical books in the world, with more than 180 titles published in six languages.

BOOK PRESENTATION

Welcome to the Psychology of Digital Persuasion journey of discovery! In this book, you will find an in-depth look at how technologies shape our decisions in the digital environment. In an increasingly connected world, the choices we make online are not only personal, but deeply influenced by algorithms, interface design and digital marketing strategies. Understanding the psychological principles that underpin these influences is essential to protect yourself and make more conscious and informed decisions. This book is an essential guide for those who want to understand the invisible forces that shape digital behavior and how to critically and ethically navigate this new landscape.

Chapter 1: Fundamentals of the Psychology of Persuasion

The first step on our journey is to understand the fundamental concepts of persuasion. In this chapter, we will address the definition and history of persuasion in psychology, as well as exploring how its classic principles have transformed with the advancement of digital technologies. Persuasion, although an essential part of human communication, has taken a new form in the digital age. Here, we will discuss how technologies amplify their effects, making persuasion faster, more effective and, often, imperceptible.

Chapter 2: Psychological Models Applied to Digital Persuasion

Digital persuasion is not a random phenomenon. On the contrary, it follows well-defined psychological models. In the second chapter, we will explore the Cialdini Model, which identifies six fundamental principles of influence, and the Fogg Model, which analyzes the intersection between technology and behavior.

Additionally, we will discuss other psychological approaches relevant to the digital environment, offering a solid foundation for understanding the complex interactions that shape our decisions online.

Chapter 3: The Impact of Personalization on Decision Making

Have you ever noticed how product, music or news suggestions seem to be tailor-made for you? This is no coincidence. In this chapter, we discuss how algorithms shape our preferences and reinforce behaviors, creating a filter bubble that can limit our view of the world. We examine the personalization strategies used by companies to influence users, highlighting both the benefits and risks of this phenomenon.

Chapter 4: Persuasive Design and the Psychology of User Experience

Digital interface design is not just an aesthetic issue; it is also a powerful tool of persuasion. Chapter 4 explores how UX (user experience) and UI (user interface) principles are designed to influence emotions and actions. We also analyze dark patterns, which are design strategies used to manipulate user behavior in questionable ethical ways, and their impacts.

Chapter 5: The Psychology of Engagement and the Attention Economy

With the proliferation of social networks and apps, attention has become a valuable currency. In this chapter, we will explore the role of dopamine in digital addiction and how platforms use this mechanism to retain users. We will also examine the positive feedback loop that keeps users engaged and the behavioral engagement mechanics that have become the foundation of many digital platforms.

Chapter 6: Persuasion and Decision Making in the Digital Environment

The decisions we make in the digital environment are deeply

influenced by emotions and heuristics. In Chapter 6, we discussed how emotional biases, such as scarcity and urgency bias, affect our decision-making online. Furthermore, we analyze the difference between automatic decisions, which are often impulsive, and deliberate decisions, which require more reflection.

Chapter 7: Neuromarketing and Subconscious Influence

Neuromarketing is a powerful tool that explores how our brains respond to specific stimuli. In this chapter, we discuss how neuromarketing uses brain triggers to influence our purchasing decisions and online behavior. We also analyze how emotion tracking methods and visual and audio stimuli are used to create persuasive experiences, often without the user realizing it.

Chapter 8: Artificial Intelligence and Algorithmic Persuasion

Artificial intelligence doesn't just anticipate our behaviors; it also shapes them. Chapter 8 explores how AI algorithms influence our choices and behaviors, with an emphasis on personalized recommendations and their psychological impact. We also discuss the ethical challenges involved in using AI to persuade users, an issue that will become increasingly relevant in the future.

Chapter 9: The Power of Stories and Persuasive Narrative

A good story can be a powerful tool in shaping our perceptions and decisions. In this chapter, we explore how narratives influence users' choices in the digital environment. Narrative psychology in marketing and social media is a widely used strategy to engage consumers and direct their actions. Here, you will learn how storytelling is used in digital persuasion and examples of how it is used effectively.

Chapter 10: Gamification and Reinforcement Psychology

Gamification is a powerful technique that uses the principles of reinforcement psychology to shape behavior. In this chapter, we look at how games and reward systems are used to increase user engagement and retention on digital platforms. Gamification is especially relevant in sectors such as education, healthcare and commerce, where its psychological impact can be profound and transformative.

Chapter 11: Social Media Persuasion: The Mass Effect

Social media has the power to create trends and shape decisions in massive ways. Chapter 11 explores how social proof – the phenomenon where people tend to follow the actions of others – influences our decision-making. We also discuss the role of digital influencers and the impact of content going viral on public perception and opinion formation.

Chapter 12: The Effect of Colors, Sounds, and Shapes on Persuasion

Visual and sound elements have a profound impact on our emotions and decisions. Chapter 12 covers how colors, shapes, and sounds are used strategically to influence the user experience. Typography, the arrangement of elements on the screen, and the use of certain sounds can trigger specific emotional responses, creating a persuasive experience.

Chapter 13: Consumer Psychology and Online Shopper Behavior

Online buyer behavior is complex and heavily influenced by psychological factors. In Chapter 13, we discuss how emotions and heuristics affect digital shopping, as well as exploring the mental triggers used in marketing strategies. We also examine the factors that influence customer loyalty and the psychological impact of digital marketing on consumption.

Chapter 14: Persuasion and Fake News: How People Are Manipulated

Fake news is a clear example of how people can be manipulated through persuasive narratives. Chapter 14 explores confirmation bias and the role of algorithms in spreading false information. We analyze the psychological strategies used to create and spread fake news and how this affects our perception of reality.

Chapter 15: Psychology of Fear and Urgency in the Digital Environment

Fear and urgency are powerful tools of persuasion. Chapter 15 examines how these emotions are used to drive immediate action on digital platforms. From marketing to the digital security industry, fear is a common tactic to influence user behaviors and accelerate their decisions.

Chapter 16: Persuasion in Digital Health and Wellbeing

Digital technologies are also used to influence behaviors related to health and well-being. In Chapter 16, we explore how mental and physical health platforms use persuasive techniques to encourage healthy habits, while also discussing the risks of digital overexposure and behavioral burnout.

Chapter 17: Digital Education and the Use of Persuasion for Engagement

Digital education is an area where persuasion plays a central role. Chapter 17 investigates how educational platforms use persuasive techniques to increase engagement and knowledge retention. We also discuss the impact of personalization on learning and how platforms adapt the experience to maximize effectiveness.

Chapter 18: Ethics and Transparency in the Psychology of Digital Persuasion

The ethical use of digital persuasion is a central theme in chapter 18. We discuss the boundary between persuasion and manipulation, the role of privacy and informed consent, and the responsible practices that companies and digital platforms must adopt to ensure fair and transparent interaction with users.

Chapter 19: How to Protect Yourself from Unwanted Persuasion

In this chapter, we provide practical strategies for increasing awareness of persuasive techniques and how to protect yourself from them. Identifying cognitive biases and digital traps is essential to maintaining autonomy in online decisions, and this chapter offers valuable tools to help the reader develop more critical and independent thinking.

Chapter 20: The Future of Digital Persuasion

The future of digital persuasion is exciting but also challenging. In the final chapter, we explore emerging technologies and new challenges for digital persuasion, including the impact of new media and neural interfaces on human influence. We conclude with a reflection on how we can develop a more conscious and ethical relationship with technology.

Final Conclusion

By the end of this book, we hope you have a clear understanding of the psychological forces that shape your digital decisions. The knowledge acquired here is not only a tool for understanding the digital world, but also an important step towards acting more consciously, critically and ethically in the digital age.

We thank you for reading and invite you to continue on this learning journey. The future of digital persuasion is in your hands.

CHAPTER 1. FUNDAMENTALS OF THE PSYCHOLOGY OF PERSUASION

Persuasion has been one of the fundamental pillars of human communication, present in various areas such as politics, marketing, relationships and, more recently, in the digital world. Your understanding goes far beyond simple convincing techniques; it is a deep psychological dynamic that influences the way people think, feel and make decisions. This chapter explores the foundations of the psychology of persuasion, its history, and how technological advances have expanded and sophisticated its effects, especially in the digital environment.

Definition and History of Persuasion in Psychology

Persuasion, in its simplest sense, can be defined as the process of influencing the attitudes, beliefs or behaviors of other people through arguments, suggestions or emotional appeals. In psychology, the study of persuasion originated with an interest in understanding how and why people are susceptible to changing their beliefs or behaviors when exposed to certain messages.

The Greek philosopher Aristotle, in his work *Rhetoric*, was one of the first to study persuasion systematically. He identified three main forms of persuasion: *ethos* (credibility of the speaker), *pathos* (emotional appeal) and *logos* (logical argumentation). These three elements remain relevant today and are fundamental to any persuasive strategy. THE *ethos* refers to the trust that the audience places in the speaker, the *pathos* concerns the ability to arouse emotions, and the *logos* involves the strength of rational arguments.

Over time, modern psychology has developed more detailed and empirical theories about persuasion, many of them centering on experimental studies that looked at the way people react to different types of messages. Among the most influential scholars, Robert Cialdini stood out with his work *Influence: The Psychology of Persuasion*, in which he presents six principles of persuasion that, to this day, are widely applied in both marketing and political communication. These principles are: reciprocity, commitment and consistency, social approval, authority, scarcity and friendliness.

In addition to Cialdini, other psychologists, such as Richard E. Petty and John Cacioppo, contributed to the Elaboration of Probability Model (ELM), which explores the two main paths of information processing: the central path (rational and logical) and the peripheral path (emotional and heuristics-based). Studying these approaches has helped build a deeper understanding of persuasion, including the interplay between reason and emotion in decision-making processes.

The Principles of Classic Persuasion and Its Evolution in the Digital Environment

In the early days, persuasion was mainly related to interpersonal communication. The evolution of persuasive psychology has occurred over time with the growing impact of traditional media, such as radio, television and, more recently, the internet. In the digital environment, the rules of persuasion have been refined, as technology offers a series of tools that amplify their effects, making persuasion more precise and, often, more effective.

Cialdini's principles apply directly to the digital context, although the way they are used has changed considerably. For example, the principle of *reciprocity*, which says that people tend to return favors or gifts received, is often used in digital marketing strategies. Offering free content, such as eBooks or software trials, can be a way of applying reciprocity, encouraging users to make purchases or share their personal data in exchange for something they received.

The principle of *scarcity*, which explores the idea that people desire more what is perceived as rare or limited, is widely used on e-commerce and social media platforms. Examples of this are limited-time offers, reduced stock, or "last units" notifications. This strategy of creating a sense of urgency makes consumers feel compelled to make quick decisions before the opportunity disappears.

How Technology Amplifies the Effects of Persuasion

The impact of technology on persuasion is multifaceted. Over the past few decades, technology has provided ways for persuasive strategies to be more targeted, personalized and, in some ways, more difficult to avoid. The amplification of the effects of persuasion occurs largely due to the massive collection of data and the development of sophisticated algorithms that analyze and predict user behaviors.

One of the most obvious ways to amplify digital persuasion is personalization. Platforms such as Facebook, Google and Amazon use user information, such as browsing history, previous purchases and declared preferences, to personalize the user experience. This not only increases the effectiveness of persuasive messages, but also creates a feedback loop that reinforces previous behaviors, creating a filter bubble where users are constantly exposed to content that aligns with their beliefs and interests.

Another important factor is the ubiquity of digital technologies. The cell phone, for example, is an extension of the modern individual, always within reach. This constant access to digital platforms creates an opportunity for companies to influence user decisions in real time. Notifications, alerts, and reminders are used to keep users engaged and persuade them to take quick actions, such as clicking links, making purchases, or interacting with content. These reminders often appeal to emotions and the fear of losing something, reinforcing the scarcity principle mentioned earlier.

Furthermore, social networks play a fundamental role in amplifying persuasion. They create a platform for social proof, one of Cialdini's principles, allowing users to see the behavior of their friends and followers. This type of exposure can lead to decisions that are more influenced by the approval of others, whether in relation to products, ideas or behaviors.

On platforms like Instagram and YouTube, digital influencers use their authority to persuade their followers to buy products or adopt specific behaviors. The trust that these influencers generate with their followers makes their recommendations much more effective than traditional marketing strategies. Furthermore, the use of algorithms to recommend content increases the relevance of persuasive messages, as the user is constantly exposed to personalized options.

Technology has also enabled the automation of persuasion. AI systems are capable of personalizing messages on a large scale and with great precision. Recommendation algorithms, like those used by Netflix and Spotify, not only suggest products and content based on a user's past behavior, but also anticipate what they would like to consume in the future. These recommendations are personalized in real time, increasing the likelihood of engagement and action.

One of the most powerful techniques is the use of gamification, which incorporates game elements, such as rewards and progression, into digital platforms to encourage engagement. Points, achievements and rankings systems are used to create a positive feedback loop that keeps users engaged and motivated to continue interacting with the platform. The use of gamification in the digital environment is a clear example of how persuasion can be applied subliminally, causing users to make decisions without realizing that they are being influenced.

The field of persuasion psychology continues to evolve as

new technologies are developed and adopted. Understanding the psychological forces behind digital persuasion becomes increasingly essential, not only for marketers, but also for consumers seeking to better understand the mechanisms that influence their decisions online. As technology becomes more sophisticated, it's important to be aware of the amplifying effects of persuasion and how it can be used both for good and to manipulate behavior in subtle but powerful ways.

From this point on, we enter a world where persuasion is no longer just a convincing technique, but an intrinsic force in the digital platforms that shape modern society. Knowing the foundations of the psychology of persuasion, how it evolves and adapts to the digital environment, is the first step to critically and consciously navigating this new scenario, helping not only to make better decisions, but also to better understand how our choices are being shaped with each click.

CHAPTER 2. PSYCHOLOGICAL MODELS APPLIED TO DIGITAL PERSUASION

The psychology of persuasion is a complex field that seeks to understand how people can be influenced to change their beliefs, attitudes or behaviors. In the digital context, the persuasive principles that govern human behavior are constantly being refined and adapted to take advantage of emerging technologies. This chapter explores two of the most influential models in the area of digital persuasion: the Cialdini Model and its six principles of influence, and the Fogg Model, which focuses on the intersection between technology and behavior. We will also discuss other psychological approaches that are essential to understanding persuasion in the digital environment.

The Cialdini Model and the Six Principles of Influence

Robert Cialdini is one of the most important names when talking about persuasion. In your work *Influence: The Psychology of Persuasion*, he defines six fundamental principles that explain how people can be persuaded effectively. These principles are based on psychological studies and observations of human behavior, and are widely used in both marketing contexts and everyday interactions. These principles are:

1. **Reciprocity**: The tendency to return favors is one of the pillars of human persuasion. Cialdini argues that, when someone does us a favor, we feel the need to reciprocate, which creates an exchange dynamic that can be explored in different persuasive strategies. In the digital context, this is often seen in marketing tactics,

where a product or service is offered free of charge (such as samples or trials), generating an implicit obligation of reciprocity on the part of the consumer.

2. **Commitment and Consistency**: Once people commit to something, be it a small action or a big decision, they tend to be consistent with that commitment, seeking to maintain coherence in their actions. In the digital environment, this can be observed in the use of "accept" buttons in contracts, or when a user interacts with content for the first time, whether subscribing to a newsletter or liking a page. These small commitments increase the likelihood of larger actions in the future, like a purchase.

3. **Social Approval**: The behavior of other people has a great influence on our own decisions. On digital platforms, social proof is often used to create a sense that something is popular or widely accepted. Product reviews, social media comments and follower numbers are clear examples of how social approval is used to increase credibility and encourage new behaviors, such as purchases or interactions.

4. **Authority**: People tend to follow those they perceive as authority figures. In the digital context, influencers, experts and companies with an established brand use their status to persuade people to trust their messages. A classic example is doctors or nutritionists who recommend health products, or celebrities who promote clothing or cosmetic brands. The trust that the audience places in these individuals makes it easier for them to accept their persuasive messages.

5. **Scarcity**: The idea that something is rare or limited increases its value in people's perception. This principle is widely used in digital marketing, with strategies such as "limited time offers" or "limited stock". Scarcity creates a sense of urgency, leading consumers to make quick decisions, often without due consideration.

6. **Sympathy**: People are more easily persuaded by those they like or identify with. In the digital environment, this principle is often explored through marketing campaigns that humanize brands, creating a friendly image that is close to the consumer. Influencers and brands that can create an emotional connection with their followers are more effective at persuasion.

These Cialdini principles are fundamental to understanding the psychology of persuasion, especially in the digital environment, where platform algorithms can be programmed to maximize the effectiveness of these strategies.

The Fogg Model and the Intersection between Technology and Behavior

The Fogg Model, developed by BJ Fogg, is a psychological approach that explores the interaction between human behavior and technology. Fogg argues that digital persuasion is not just a matter of applying psychological principles, but also involves how technology shapes users' behavior.

Fogg's model is based on three main factors that affect behavior: motivation, ability and triggers. These three elements need to be present and interact appropriately for the desired behavior to be achieved. These factors can be described as follows:

1. **Motivation**: Motivation is the force that drives a person to act. In the digital context, motivation can be generated by a series of factors, such as financial rewards, the search for social status, the need to solve a problem or even the search for entertainment. Motivation is one of the main factors that drive user behavior on digital platforms, such as social networks, e-commerce or gaming applications.

2. **Capacity**: Capability refers to the ease with which an individual can perform an action. The simpler a task is, the more likely it is to be accomplished. Fogg

highlights that technology should be designed to make actions as easy as possible. A good example of this are the simplified checkout processes on e-commerce platforms, which minimize steps and make purchasing easier. Capacity is also affected by factors such as the user's familiarity with the technology and the accessibility of the interface.

3. **Triggers**: Triggers are the stimuli that trigger the desired action. They can be internal, like a feeling of urgency or desire, or external, like a push notification on your cell phone. Fogg argues that the interplay between motivation, ability and triggers is crucial to user behavior. For example, a push notification (trigger) that notifies you that an item is discounted (reason) and offers an easy purchase (ability) can be an effective trigger for an impulsive purchase.

According to the Fogg Model, the combination of these three elements creates a "desired behavior." The theory is applied in a wide range of digital situations, such as the design of apps, websites and social media platforms. Understanding how to effectively manipulate these three factors is critical to creating successful digital persuasion strategies.

Other Psychological Approaches Relevant to the Digital Environment

In addition to Cialdini and Fogg's models, there are other psychological approaches that are relevant to understanding digital persuasion. These approaches focus on different aspects of human behavior, including emotions, social cognition, and the psychology of decisions.

1. **Dual Persuasion Theory (Probability Elaboration Model - ELM)**: Dual persuasion theory, proposed by Richard Petty and John Cacioppo, suggests that there are two main ways of processing information: the central pathway and the peripheral pathway. In the

central path, individuals process the message in a logical and detailed way, while in the peripheral path, decisions are influenced by external factors, such as the attractiveness of the presenter or the amount of superficial information. In the digital context, the peripheral path is often used in visual advertisements, where the aesthetics and status of the presenter are more important than the actual content of the message.

2. **Social Cognition Theory**: Social cognition, as proposed by Albert Bandura, highlights the importance of social influences in the formation of attitudes and behaviors. Social learning theory suggests that people learn by observing others, and this is particularly relevant to the digital environment, where the behavior of influencers and celebrities can have a significant impact on followers' decisions. Platforms like Instagram and TikTok use social cognition theory to create a positive feedback loop in which users imitate behaviors they see as popular or rewarded.

3. **The Psychology of Quick Decisions**: The psychology of quick decisions, also known as heuristics, refers to the use of "mental shortcuts" that allow people to make quick, efficient decisions. In the digital environment, heuristics are often applied through interface design techniques such as visible "action buttons" and vibrant colors that encourage quick decision-making. An example of this are "buy now" buttons on e-commerce sites, which trigger a purchasing decision with minimal thought.

The psychological models presented in this chapter provide a detailed understanding of how digital persuasion works, from basic principles to more complex interactions between technology and human behavior. The Cialdini Model, with its six principles of influence, offers a solid basis for understanding persuasive strategies applied in digital environments. The Fogg Model expands this understanding by integrating technological and behavioral factors, revealing how motivation, capacity and triggers interact to shape user behavior.

In addition to these models, additional approaches such as dual persuasion theory, social cognition, and quick decision heuristics show how psychologists have expanded our understanding of the forces that influence choices in the digital world. Understanding these theories is essential for any professional who wants to create effective persuasion strategies, whether in marketing, digital product design or political communication.

These models not only provide a solid theoretical foundation, but also offer practical insights for applying the psychology of persuasion in an increasingly sophisticated and interconnected digital world.

CHAPTER 3. THE IMPACT OF PERSONALIZATION ON DECISION MAKING

Personalization plays a crucial role in the modern digital landscape. With the advancement of technologies, the ability to adapt products, services and experiences to individual preferences has become a central strategy for companies and digital platforms. However, while personalization can improve the user experience, it also raises questions about the impact on consumer decisions and the potential risks associated with this process. Digital personalization is not just about convenience; it is often used to influence purchasing behaviors and even shape individuals' beliefs and attitudes. This chapter explores how algorithms shape preferences and reinforce behaviors, the creation of filter bubbles and the risks associated with excessive personalization, and the strategies used by companies to personalize the user experience and influence user decisions.

How Algorithms Shape Preferences and Reinforce Behaviors

In recent years, personalization has increasingly been shaped by algorithms that collect and analyze large volumes of data to predict and influence user preferences. These algorithms are designed to identify behavior patterns, analyze past interactions and, based on this data, suggest products, services or content that are more likely to please the user. The goal is to make the experience more relevant and, ultimately, increase engagement and conversion rates.

Personalization algorithms operate through a continuous cycle of data collection, analysis, and adjustment of recommendations.

E-commerce platforms, social networks, streaming services and search engines, among others, use these algorithms to keep users more engaged and, consequently, more likely to take an action, such as making a purchase or interacting with content.

1. **Data Collection**: The first step in the personalization process is collecting data about user behavior. This includes explicit data, such as information provided by the user (e.g. age, purchasing preferences), and implicit data, such as browsing history, time spent on different pages and clicks made on a website.

2. **Data Analysis**: Once collected, the data is analyzed using machine learning and artificial intelligence techniques. The objective is to identify patterns of behavior and predict future actions. Algorithms can, for example, identify that a user who frequently searches for technology books is likely to be interested in new releases in this genre.

3. **Customizing Reactions**: Based on predictions made by algorithms, platforms offer personalized recommendations. These recommendations can range from simple product suggestions to specific content creation. For example, on an e-commerce site, a user who recently purchased a cell phone may receive suggestions for compatible accessories, such as covers and headphones.

4. **Feedback and Adjustment**: The personalization cycle closes with user feedback. Actions taken (such as a purchase or viewing content) are analyzed again to adjust future recommendations. This creates a dynamic and constantly evolving system that seeks to make suggestions increasingly precise.

This form of personalization helps increase the relevance of offers presented to users, but can also have effects on consumer behavior. Over time, users may begin to feel increasingly driven by these recommendations, especially as algorithms become more effective at predicting and shaping their choices. Continuous engagement with this personalized content reinforces certain behaviors and preferences, creating a vicious cycle where past behavior is constantly reinforced by suggestions.

The Filter Bubble and the Risks of Excessive Personalization

The filter bubble is a concept that describes the digital isolation caused by excessive personalization. In simple terms, a filter bubble occurs when personalization algorithms begin showing users only information that confirms their previous beliefs or preferences, excluding opposing views or new content that could challenge those opinions.

1. **The Filter Bubble Mechanism**: This phenomenon occurs because algorithms often prioritize what has already been consumed. Platforms such as social networks and search engines use filters to decide which information is most relevant to each user, based on their previous behavior. This creates a situation where the user is constantly exposed to the same type of content, reinforcing their existing beliefs or preferences.

2. **Impacts on Behavior and Perception**: The filter bubble has significant implications for user behavior and perception. When people are continually exposed to a limited set of ideas or products, their worldview becomes increasingly narrow and polarized. This phenomenon can affect areas such as politics, where continuous exposure to content that reinforces a certain ideology can lead to a more radicalized view.

3. **Exclusion of Alternatives and Limitation of Choices**: Excessive customization can also lead to the exclusion of important alternatives. When platforms focus on only showing what a user already likes or has consumed, they often fail to present new options or perspectives that could be of interest. This not only limits the user's choices, but can also cause them to miss opportunities

to discover new products or ideas.

4. **Impacts on the Decision Process**: The filter bubble can also affect how people make decisions. Continuous exposure to a narrow set of options can cause users to make decisions based on a reduced number of alternatives, without considering all available options. This can result in less informed or impulsive choices, which are heavily influenced by algorithm suggestions.

Personalization Strategies Used by Companies to Influence Users

Companies and digital platforms have used various personalization strategies to influence users' decisions, with the aim of increasing engagement and conversions. These strategies can be divided into a few main categories:

1. **Recommendations Based on Behavioral Data**: Recommendations based on past user behavior are one of the most common strategies. These systems analyze browsing history, previous purchases and interactions with content to suggest new products or services. In the case of streaming platforms, for example, film and series suggestions are made based on what the user has previously watched. These recommendations increase the likelihood that the user will continue using the service, as the offers presented are more relevant to their tastes and interests.

2. **Customization of Prices and Offers**: Some platforms use behavioral data to personalize prices or offers in order to increase the chances of conversion. This can include personalized discounts based on a user's purchasing frequency or total amount spent. Price personalization is a powerful strategy because it makes the user feel like they are receiving an exclusive or advantageous offer, which can influence their purchasing decision.

3. **A/B Testing for Interface Optimization**: A/B testing is a

widely used technique to optimize user experience and improve conversion rates. Companies use this technique to test different versions of a page, layout or call to action and see which one generates better results. For example, a company might test two versions of a buy button to see which results in more clicks, adjusting the pages based on the test results. A/B testing helps you continually refine personalization and increase the effectiveness of persuasive strategies.

4. **Gamification and Personalized Rewards**: Gamification is another strategy used by companies to keep users engaged. This involves using game elements such as scoring, badges and levels to encourage desired behavior. Personalized rewards are offered based on the user's past actions. For example, a customer who has purchased several times in an e-commerce can receive a "VIP customer" status and access exclusive promotions, encouraging them to continue purchasing.

5. **Real-Time Personalization**: Some platforms are able to personalize the user experience in real time, based on the interactions that are currently taking place. This could include dynamically changing promotional banners, adjusting product recommendations, or sending personalized messages via notifications. Real-time personalization creates a sense of exclusivity and urgency as the content shown to the user is constantly updated according to their current actions.

Personalization has a profound impact on decision-making in the digital environment, shaping users' preferences and influencing their behaviors in complex ways. Using algorithms to personalize the experience, while bringing benefits in terms of relevance and convenience, also raises concerns about the risks of filter bubbles and excessive personalization. Creating feedback loops in which user behaviors are constantly reinforced can lead to a limited view of the world, negatively impacting the diversity of options and the quality of decisions.

On the other hand, personalization strategies used by companies have shown to be effective in increasing engagement and conversions, while creating a more personalized experience adapted to users' needs. However, it is essential that companies and platforms take an ethical and transparent approach when applying personalization, to prevent the user experience from becoming overly manipulative or restrictive. Digital personalization, when done in a balanced and responsible way, can bring significant benefits to both users and companies.

CHAPTER 4. PERSUASIVE DESIGN AND THE PSYCHOLOGY OF USER EXPERIENCE

User experience (UX) and user interface (UI) have become increasingly focused on maximizing engagement and conversion. Persuasive design uses principles of psychology to create experiences that shape users' decisions, encouraging them to act in specific ways. This approach involves applying techniques that influence emotions, reactions and behaviors without the user realizing it, often leading them to take actions that they might not otherwise have taken. While persuasive design is effective in improving user experience, it can also be problematic when used in a manipulative way. This chapter explores how UX and UI elements are designed to influence emotions and actions, the phenomenon of dark patterns, and the ethical impact of digital persuasion, as well as examples of interfaces designed for engagement and conversion.

How UX and UI Are Designed to Influence Emotions and Actions

UX and UI design is an essentially user-centric field. Its main function is to ensure that the user has a pleasant and efficient experience when interacting with digital products. However, in addition to ensuring fluid and intuitive navigation, the design can also be shaped to directly influence the user's emotions and actions, creating an environment in which their choices are guided in a subtle way.

1. **Psychological Principles in Design**: UX and UI designers often apply principles from psychology

to increase design effectiveness. This involves understanding how users perceive information, how they make decisions, and what motivates them to act. The psychology of colors, the use of shapes, spacing and even the choice of words can trigger emotional responses that directly influence user behavior.

2. **The Psychology of Colors**: Colors play a significant role in creating an emotional atmosphere. Colors like red can evoke urgency or excitement, while blue conveys confidence and calm. When combined appropriately, these colors can be used to induce certain emotions that influence purchasing or engagement decisions. For example, a "buy now" button on an e-commerce site often uses vibrant colors like green or red to generate a sense of urgency or immediate action.

3. **A Lei by Hick-Hyman**: Hick-Hyman's Law is a fundamental concept in UX, which states that the amount of time needed to make a decision increases with the number of options. In user interfaces, this means fewer options and simplified navigation often result in faster, more effective decisions. The design can be structured to present only the most relevant options or simplify the navigation flow to reduce the user's cognitive burden.

4. **Principle of Reciprocity**: This psychological principle is based on the idea that people tend to return favors. In design, this can be applied by offering something for free, such as exclusive content, discounts or extra features, with the aim of making the user feel an obligation to reciprocate, often by making a purchase or subscribing to a service. E-commerce sites and subscription platforms often offer free trials or exclusive content as a way to induce action.

5. **Scarcity and Urgency**: Scarcity is another psychological principle that is widely used in interface design. When a product or offer is perceived as rare or available for a

limited time, users tend to act more impulsively. Sites often use phrases like "Only 3 items left" or "Offer valid until midnight" to create a sense of urgency that motivates users to act quickly without in-depth thought.

6. **Anchoring**: The concept of anchoring is another psychological principle that is used in interface design. This principle involves displaying an initially higher priced option (such as a luxury item) so that subsequent options appear more affordable in comparison. This can be seen in pricing models, where the price of a product or service is positioned alongside a higher original price to give the impression that the offer is advantageous.

Dark Patterns and the Ethical Impact of Digital Persuasion

While digital persuasion can be a powerful and legitimate tool for influencing user experience and improving engagement, there are practices that can cross ethical lines. Dark patterns refer to intentionally manipulative design techniques that are designed to trick users or cause them to make decisions that they would not have chosen if they knew exactly what was happening.

1. **Defining Dark Patterns**: Dark patterns are design practices that manipulate users into taking actions they would not have done if they were fully informed about the process. This may include displaying options in a way that confuses the user, hides important information, or makes it more difficult for the user to undo an action (such as canceling a subscription).

2. **Common Examples of Obscure Patterns**:

- **Charging for something unsolicited**: Many platforms offer free trials, but after a period of time, they start charging for a service without clear communication that this will occur. Additionally, users often have to go the extra mile to cancel their subscription before they are charged.

- o **Deselecting privacy options**: Some platforms leave the consent boxes for data sharing pre-checked, forcing the user to uncheck them if they do not want their information to be shared. This can be considered a form of manipulation, as many people simply ignore these boxes and end up sharing more data than they would like.
- o **"Cancellation Confusion"**: Intentionally making the process of canceling a subscription or service difficult or confusing is a common practice on some websites. This may include multiple steps, complex forms, or a cluttered interface that makes it difficult for the user to find the cancellation option.

3. **Ethical Impact**: The practice of using dark standards can have serious consequences for the companies and platforms that use them. While these tactics may generate an immediate increase in conversions or subscriptions, they erode user trust and harm your brand reputation in the long run. The ethics of digital design imply creating interfaces that are not only effective, but also respect the rights and autonomy of users. Excessive use of dark standards can result in brand image damage, legal problems, and a less transparent and fair online environment.

4. **Regulations and Transparency**: In response to the increase in dark standards, several regulations have been implemented to protect consumers. The European Union, for example, has been a leader in creating legislation such as the General Data Protection Regulation (GDPR), which requires websites to be more transparent about their use of data and offer users control over their information. Regulation seeks to ensure that digital design is more transparent and less manipulative.

Examples of Interfaces Designed for

Engagement and Conversion

Several digital platforms use design strategies to maximize engagement and increase conversion rates, applying persuasion techniques in an ethical or manipulative way. The following are examples of how interfaces are designed to keep users engaged and likely to take specific actions.

1. **E-commerce sites**: Most e-commerce websites aggressively apply persuasive design to encourage users to make quick purchasing decisions. "Quick Buy" buttons are highlighted, with vibrant colors and phrases like "Limited Stock" or "Last Units", creating a sense of urgency. Additionally, many sites feature "Product Recommendations" based on the user's browsing history, making the user feel like they are making an informed choice when adding items to their cart.

2. **Streaming platforms**: Platforms like Netflix and Spotify use design techniques to keep users engaged. Well-designed interfaces make it easy for users to discover new content, with personalized recommendations based on their viewing or listening history. The interfaces often highlight new releases or offer exclusive content to subscribers, encouraging users to stay on the platform and consume more content.

3. **Social Media Applications**: Social networks like Facebook, Instagram and Twitter are highly dependent on design strategies to ensure users stay engaged as long as possible. The use of personalized notifications, feeds updated in real time and the creation of "feedback loops" (where the user is rewarded with likes and comments, encouraging more interactions) are widely used techniques to create an addictive experience.

4. **Subscription Services**: Services like Amazon Prime or Spotify Premium offer highly persuasive design interfaces, with an emphasis on the benefits of a paid subscription. Interfaces are designed to highlight the

uniqueness and additional functionality users will have access to, creating a sense of value and urgency to sign up.

Persuasive UX and UI design is not only a tool for improving user experience, but also a powerful mechanism for influencing decisions and behaviors. While persuasion techniques can be beneficial for increasing engagement and conversion, it is crucial that designers take an ethical approach when applying these strategies. Dark patterns may yield immediate results, but in the long term, they undermine user trust and loyalty. As digital design continues to evolve, it will become increasingly important to balance persuasion and ethics to create experiences that are beneficial to both users and businesses.

CHAPTER 5. THE PSYCHOLOGY OF ENGAGEMENT AND THE ATTENTION ECONOMY

With the increased use of digital devices and the proliferation of social networks, the impact of engagement psychology in creating platforms designed to capture and retain users' attention has become evident. The design of such platforms is deeply rooted in understanding the human mind, especially how it reacts to stimuli and rewards. This chapter explores the crucial role of dopamine in digital addiction, how social networks use the mechanics of behavioral engagement to increase screen time and user retention, and how the positive feedback loop is implemented across platforms to maximize engagement.

The Role of Dopamine in Digital Addiction and User Retention

Dopamine is a fundamental neurotransmitter for human motivation and pleasure. It plays a central role in the brain's reward system, and its release is closely associated with feelings of pleasure, satisfaction and motivation. In the digital context, dopamine is released every time a user receives a reward, such as a notification, a "like" on a post, a message or even when consuming content that they find interesting.

1. **Dopamine and Instant Rewards**: The continuous use of digital platforms is based on delivering instant rewards that activate the dopamine system in the brain. A user's interaction with a platform, such as viewing posts, commenting or sharing content, generates small doses of dopamine, creating a feeling of immediate gratification. This, in turn, reinforces user behavior,

encouraging them to repeat these actions constantly.

2. **The Effect of Intermittent Rewards**: One of the most effective ways to maintain user engagement on digital platforms is the use of intermittent rewards, i.e. rewards that are not delivered consistently but in an unpredictable manner. This type of reward is known to be highly addictive, as the human brain responds with a more intense release of dopamine when a reward is not guaranteed, but is achieved after effort or expectation. On social networks, this is reflected in notifications that appear sporadically, such as new "likes", comments or followers.

3. **Notifications and the Addiction Cycle**: The practice of constantly sending notifications is one of the most powerful strategies used to keep users engaged. Each notification serves as a stimulus that activates the reward system in the brain, making the user feel the need to check their cell phone or access the platform to check the reward. This repetitive cycle of stimuli and rewards strengthens the behavior, creating a digital addiction similar to that seen in addictive behaviors, such as gambling.

4. **Impact on User Retention**: The release of dopamine not only keeps users engaged, but is also a crucial factor in retention. Platforms that can stimulate this system effectively are more likely to keep their users active for long periods of time. Constant engagement, generated by dopamine rewards, can lead users to spend more time on the platform, checking notifications, consuming more content and interacting in different ways, resulting in greater retention.

Social Networks and the Mechanics of Behavioral Engagement

Social networks are classic examples of platforms that deeply explore the psychology of behavioral engagement. Each has been carefully designed to encourage continued use, create emotional dependency, and maximize users' interaction with the platform.

1. **Content Feed and Algorithmic Curation**: The content feed of platforms like Instagram, Facebook and Twitter is one of the main things responsible for keeping the user engaged. These platforms use sophisticated algorithms to select and display content that will maximize the likelihood that the user will interact with what is shown. Algorithms analyze a user's past behavior, such as likes, comments and shares, to predict the type of content they will find most interesting. This continuous personalization increases the likelihood that the user will consume more content and therefore stay on the platform longer.

2. **Social Interactions and Public Recognition**: Social recognition is a powerful motivation for engagement on digital platforms. Social networks encourage users to interact and share content, often through "likes", comments or shares. This recognition, often public, generates a feeling of social approval, which activates reward mechanisms in the brain and motivates users to continue creating content, publishing photos or commenting on others' posts. The more "engagement" a user receives, the more they are incentivized to continue contributing to the platform.

3. **The Challenge of FOMO (Fear of Missing Out)**: The fear of missing out, or FOMO (Fear of Missing Out), is another element that social networks exploit to keep users engaged. Platforms are designed to create a sense of urgency and exclusivity, where users feel they need to be constantly connected so they don't miss relevant events, updates or news. This is reinforced by constant notifications, new posts and alerts, creating a cycle in which the user feels the need to stay "present" so as not to be excluded from discussions or interactions.

4. **Gamification and Social Challenges**: Gamification, the

practice of applying game mechanics to non-game platforms, is a widely used strategy for engaging users. This can include creating challenges, badges, rankings and virtual rewards. Platforms like Snapchat and Instagram, for example, use "trophies" or "badges" as a form of recognition, which creates a sense of achievement. This type of mechanic creates a cycle in which the user is motivated to continue interacting and completing tasks to earn more rewards, further fueling digital addiction.

The Positive Feedback Cycle and Its Application on Various Platforms

The positive feedback loop is a fundamental concept in the design of digital platforms, especially on social media. It occurs when a user action results in a response that reinforces that same action, creating a continuous loop that keeps the user engaged with the platform. This cycle is widely used on many of the platforms we use daily.

1. **News Feed and Instant Feedback**: The news feed of platforms like Facebook or Twitter is an excellent example of how the positive feedback loop is implemented. Whenever the user interacts with the platform (liking, commenting, sharing), he receives an immediate response, such as a "likes" or "comments" notification. This generates a feeling of validation and reward, which motivates the user to continue interacting, fueling the cycle.

2. **Video Platforms and Visual Rewards**: Video sharing platforms like YouTube and TikTok make use of positive feedback loops by displaying views, likes, and comments in real time. Each new audience interaction with a user's video generates a new emotional reward, encouraging the creator to post more content and interact more with others. The reward is clear and immediate, and

the continuous reinforcement process keeps the user increasingly engaged.

3. **Engagement Notifications**: The positive feedback loop is also driven by notifications, which are often used on messaging platforms like WhatsApp, Telegram and Snapchat. Every time a user receives a message, view, or any type of interaction, they are motivated to respond or interact again. These notifications create a continuous cycle of engagement as the user feels the need to respond to keep interactions flowing.

4. **Online Shopping Platforms and Immediate Feedback**: The positive feedback loop is also used on online shopping platforms. When making a purchase, the user receives immediate confirmation, and often, a series of product suggestions based on their purchase history. Personalized recommendation is direct feedback that reinforces purchasing behavior, motivating the user to continue purchasing.

Digital engagement is a highly psychological phenomenon, with platforms designed to explore the nuances of the human mind. Dopamine, playing a crucial role in digital addiction, encourages repetitive behavior and creates an ongoing need for reward. Social networks use behavioral mechanics like algorithmic curation, public awareness, and FOMO to create an engagement cycle that keeps users engaged. Through the positive feedback loop, platforms encourage users to constantly interact, creating a network of rewards and validation that fuels repetitive behavior. While these strategies are extremely effective at retaining users and increasing engagement, they also raise questions about the impact of digital addiction and the ethics of platform design, especially when these practices are used in manipulative ways to maximize screen time and profits.

CHAPTER 6. PERSUASION AND DECISION MAKING IN THE DIGITAL ENVIRONMENT

The digital era has brought with it a new field of study on how emotions and external stimuli influence users' behavior on the web. Digital platforms, especially social networks, online stores and applications, are increasingly sophisticated in the use of persuasive tactics that directly affect the way we make decisions. Whether clicking on an ad, making a purchase or even choosing content to consume, online decisions are not just logical or rational; they are deeply linked to emotional and psychological factors. This chapter explores the psychological mechanisms that shape decision-making in the digital environment, including the impact of emotions, scarcity bias, urgency, and the difference between automatic and deliberate decisions.

How Emotions Affect the Way We Make Decisions Online

Emotions play a crucial role in decisions made in the digital environment. When we access the internet, we are constantly exposed to stimuli that generate emotional reactions, which can impact the way we interact with content and make decisions. Digital platforms exploit this vulnerability by building experiences that trigger specific emotions, such as pleasure, fear, anger or desire, to drive user behavior.

1. **The Impact of Emotions on Online Shopping**: The digital shopping experience is not just about the rational evaluation of a product but also involves emotions. E-commerce website design, for example, is often designed to create an emotional experience that

induces consumers to make impulsive decisions. The use of images, descriptions and even ease of navigation are elements that not only inform the user, but also appeal to their emotional state. In many cases, consumers buy products not because they need them, but because the shopping experience itself makes them feel like they are doing something pleasurable, or solving an immediate emotional need.

2. **The Thrill of Exclusivity**: When a website or digital platform creates the feeling that something is exclusive or rare, it activates a feeling of desire and urgency. For example, when an online store displays a limited offer or a reduced amount of stock, it creates emotional pressure that can lead to quick, non-rational decisions. Consumers, driven by the fear of missing a unique opportunity, end up making impulsive decisions, without adequately reflecting on the real need for the product.

3. **Fear and Anxiety as Motivators**: Another example of how emotions impact decisions online is the use of messages that evoke fear or anxiety. Ad platforms, for example, often use phrases like "last units," "offer expires in 10 minutes," or "now or never" to create a sense of urgency that triggers emotions of fear and uncertainty in the consumer. This fear of missing an opportunity creates an impulse to make a quick decision, even if that decision isn't the best one in the long term.

4. **The Thrill of Instant Gratification**: Social networks are masters at creating experiences that provoke an immediate sense of gratification. Likes, comments and shares offer instant rewards that generate a release of dopamine in the brain, creating a positive feedback loop that drives users to continue browsing and interacting. This cycle is highly emotional, as users associate immediate gratification with a feeling of

social validation, increasing the likelihood of continued engagement.

The Scarcity and Urgency Bias in Digital Purchases and Interactions

Scarcity bias is a psychological phenomenon widely explored in the design of digital platforms. Scarcity, both in terms of products and time, creates a sense of urgency that changes the way we make decisions.

1. **Product Shortage**: On many e-commerce platforms, products are displayed with the indication that there are few units left in stock. This type of communication activates scarcity bias, causing the consumer to perceive the item as more valuable or desirable due to its limited availability. The fear of missing the opportunity to acquire something considered rare can induce quick and thoughtless decisions, leading consumers to buy something they were not planning to, simply because they feel that the opportunity may not be repeated.

2. **Shortage of Time**: Another type of scarcity used on digital platforms is the scarcity of time. "Limited time offer", "last hours to buy" or "exclusive discount until midnight" ads are common strategies on e-commerce sites, but also on subscription services and digital offers. When consumers are pressed by time constraints, they tend to act quickly, often ignoring logic and reflection. This urgency strategy is effective because the human brain has a tendency to place more value on what can be lost in a short period of time compared to what is available for a longer period of time.

3. **Urgency in Social Media**: On social platforms, urgency not only manifests itself in sales, but also in interactions. Notifications of new posts, updates, and interactions are designed to create a sense of urgency and exclusivity. Users who don't interact quickly may

feel like they're missing out on something important, whether it's relevant information or social interaction. This feeling of urgency leads to impulsive behavior and a decision to act immediately to "not miss" something.

4. **Scarcity Marketing and Impulsive Decisions**: Scarcity bias, when combined with urgency, creates an environment conducive to impulsive decision-making. The "stock almost sold out" or "last units" messages not only activate the fear of missing out, but also generate psychological pressure that prevents the consumer from adequately reflecting on the purchase. This type of marketing is effective because people tend to value more what is perceived as scarce or exclusive, even if that value is not real.

Automatic Decisions vs. Deliberate Decisions in the Digital Context

Decision making in the digital environment can be divided into two main types: automatic decisions and deliberate decisions. Both forms of decisions are impacted by different factors, and digital platforms explore these two types of decisions to maximize user engagement and conversion.

1. **Automatic Decisions**: Automatic decisions occur when the brain makes a quick decision without deep reflection. These decisions are often impulsive and based on habitual patterns or emotional stimuli, like the automatic responses we see on social media when we like a post without thinking much about it. The design of digital platforms is largely geared toward encouraging these quick decisions. Notifications, alerts, and personalized content curation are designed to induce automatic responses, prompting users to interact with content without conscious analysis. The absence of cognitive barriers to these decisions is one of the reasons why social networks and e-commerce sites

work so well in terms of engagement.

2. **Deliberate Decisions**: Unlike automatic decisions, deliberate decisions involve a more conscious and analytical process. The user takes the time necessary to reflect on their options, evaluate the pros and cons and make a more rational decision. Although deliberate decisions are less frequent on digital platforms, they occur in specific contexts, such as purchasing a high-value product or subscribing to a service. In these cases, the user can spend more time considering alternatives, researching and comparing prices before making the decision. However, digital platforms attempt to reduce the space for deliberate decisions, creating shopping and interaction experiences that maximize convenience and minimize the need for reflection.

3. **The Convergence of Automatic and Deliberate Decisions**: In many situations, digital platforms attempt to combine elements of automatic and deliberate decisions. For example, when a user browses an online store, they may initially be guided by automatic decisions, quickly clicking on items based on attractive images or algorithmic recommendations. However, if he is purchasing a more expensive or important item, he may move to a more deliberate decision by comparing options and reading reviews. The goal of platforms is to facilitate this process, making quick decisions as easy as possible, but also offering space for more informed decisions when necessary.

4. **Persuasion in Deliberate Decisions**: Even in more deliberate decisions, digital platforms still employ persuasion techniques. In the case of a deliberate purchase, the platform may present a "limited time discount" or an "exclusive offer" to encourage a quick decision. The use of social evidence, such as reviews from other consumers and testimonials, also aims to influence the decision in a more considered way. The

goal is to make the shopping experience more fluid by reducing the amount of time needed to make a decision, even when that decision involves more careful analysis.

Persuasion in the digital environment is an art that combines psychology, design and emotion. The impact of emotions on online decisions, scarcity bias, urgency and the difference between automatic and deliberate decisions are crucial aspects that platforms explore to maximize engagement and conversions. Emotions profoundly affect how we interact with platforms, whether through immediate gratification or the fear of losing something valuable. Scarcity bias and urgency create an environment conducive to quick and impulsive decisions, while automatic and deliberate decisions demonstrate how platforms attempt to influence user behavior in different ways. Understanding these persuasion mechanisms is essential for anyone who wants to develop more effective digital platforms and, at the same time, be more aware of the psychological impacts they can have on users.

CHAPTER 7. NEUROMARKETING AND SUBCONSCIOUS INFLUENCE

Neuromarketing is an emerging field that explores the intersection of marketing and neuroscience, using a deep understanding of human behavior to optimize marketing and sales strategies. This field is based on the idea that most consumer decisions occur at subconscious levels, being shaped by sensory and emotional stimuli that escape the consumer's conscious control. Companies that master neuromarketing techniques can create much more effective advertising campaigns and shopping experiences, influencing not only behavior, but also consumers' perceptions, emotions and attitudes. This chapter explores how neuromarketing uses brain triggers to influence decisions, emotion tracking methods in digital marketing, and the impact of visual and audio stimuli on persuasion.

How Neuromarketing Uses Brain Triggers to Influence Decisions

Neuromarketing is based on understanding how the human brain reacts to certain stimuli, seeking to use this knowledge to subtly influence consumer choices. The human brain is naturally inclined to make quick and automatic decisions, often without due reflection. Behind these decisions, there are several areas of the brain that are activated in response to specific stimuli, and understanding how these triggers work is essential to developing effective marketing strategies.

1. **Reward and Pleasure Triggers**: The brain's reward system, which involves the release of dopamine, is one of the main targets of neuromarketing. When a consumer experiences something pleasurable, such

as a discount, an instant reward or even a positive social interaction, the brain releases dopamine, which generates a feeling of pleasure and satisfaction. This mechanism can be exploited in advertising campaigns that offer immediate gratification, such as promotions, limited-time offers or loyalty programs. The pleasure generated by these rewards can cause consumers to make quick and impulsive decisions, without going through a conscious evaluation process.

2. **Triggers of Fear and Urgency**: The fear of missing an opportunity is another powerful brain trigger used in neuromarketing. This mechanism is directly related to the human survival instinct, which is driven by the need to avoid scarcity. When an offer is presented as limited in time or with restricted availability, the brain goes into alert, activating the amygdala region, associated with the processing of emotions such as fear. The fear of losing something valuable can lead consumers to make quick, impulsive decisions, purchasing products or services without in-depth analysis. Tactics like "last units in stock" or "offer valid until midnight" are widely used to exploit this trigger.

3. **Triggers of Exclusivity and Belonging**: The desire to feel part of a group or to have access to something exclusive is another trigger that can be explored in neuromarketing. The human brain is highly influenced by the need to belong, which is a fundamental need for most people. Brands that offer exclusive products or experiences, like limited editions or early access to new releases, activate this need to belong. Furthermore, by associating the brand or product with a specific group, companies can strengthen the emotional bond between the consumer and the product, encouraging purchases based on the desire to be part of a privileged circle.

4. **Positive Emotion Triggers and Association**: The human brain tends to make decisions based on

emotions, and these emotions can often be associated with brands and products. Brands that manage to create a positive emotional association, whether through a touching story, a social cause or a well-defined identity, are more likely to generate a lasting connection with their consumers. Advertising campaigns that use positive emotions, such as happiness, nostalgia or hope, can be very effective in generating an emotional response that motivates purchase. This emotional connection can be even more powerful when people feel like they are supporting something that shares their values.

Emotion Tracking Methods and Their Use in Digital Marketing

Understanding consumer emotions is an essential part of neuromarketing. In recent years, emotion tracking technologies have become more accessible, allowing brands to better understand how consumers respond to different stimuli in real time. This understanding is crucial for optimizing advertising campaigns and improving the user experience on digital platforms.

1. **Facial Expression Tracking**: One of the most common ways to track a consumer's emotions is through facial expression recognition. This technology uses cameras to capture facial microexpressions, which are quick, subtle movements that reveal a person's emotional state. Facial expressions can indicate feelings such as happiness, surprise, sadness, anger or fear, and tracking these expressions allows companies to know exactly how consumers are reacting to an ad, website or digital interaction. Neuromarketing uses this technology to adjust advertising campaigns in real time, ensuring that ads generate the desired emotional response.

2. **Eye-Tracking**: Eye-tracking is a technology that maps a consumer's eye movements as they interact with

a website or an advertisement. This technology is valuable for understanding which parts of a page attract the most attention and how users visually process information. In digital marketing, eye-tracking is used to optimize the layout of sales pages, advertisements and content, ensuring that the most important elements, such as purchase buttons or calls to action, are strategically positioned to maximize attention and interaction.

3. **Brain Activity Monitoring (Neurofeedback)**: Neurofeedback is a technique that allows you to monitor the electrical activity of the brain and thus understand how it reacts to different stimuli. In neuromarketing, neurofeedback can be used to identify which types of advertisements or website designs activate certain areas of the brain, such as those associated with pleasure, interest, or desire. This technology is particularly useful for testing advertising campaigns before launch, helping companies optimize their strategies based on accurate data on consumers' brain responses.

4. **Social Media Data Analysis**: Social media is a fertile field for tracking emotions, as user interactions on the platforms provide a rich set of data about how people feel about brands, products and campaigns. Sentiment analysis tools are used to analyze shared content, comments and user reactions, identifying emotional patterns. By monitoring these sentiments in real time, companies can adjust their marketing approach to create greater emotional resonance with their audiences.

5. **The Application of Emotional Data in Digital Marketing**: Using these technologies, brands can create highly personalized campaigns that speak directly to consumers' feelings. By identifying the most common emotions associated with a product or service,

companies can tailor their ads, offers and experiences to evoke the emotional responses that encourage action, whether it's a purchase, click or sign-up.

The Role of Visual and Sound Stimuli in Persuasion

Visual and sound stimuli play a crucial role in the digital persuasion process. The human brain is extremely sensitive to sensory stimuli, and both vision and hearing play a central role in how we process information and make decisions. Visual design and sound are used in neuromarketing to create an immersive environment that stimulates emotions and facilitates the purchase or interaction decision.

1. **Visual Stimuli**: The visual design of a sales page, an advertisement or a website can directly influence the consumer's perception and decision. Colors, shapes and layouts are selected based on knowledge about how they affect consumer psychology. Warm colors, like red and orange, are often used to generate a sense of urgency and excitement, while cool colors, like blue and green, are associated with feelings of calm and confidence. The appropriate use of colors can make the consumer feel attracted or even calm, depending on the objective of the campaign. Additionally, visual composition, contrast between elements, and balance of information are crucial to ensuring that the most important elements, such as calls to action or special offers, are highlighted effectively.

2. **Sound Stimuli**: Sound also plays a significant role in neuromarketing. Music and sound effects are used to create a specific emotional atmosphere, influencing consumer behavior. Pleasant or calming sounds can generate a feeling of comfort and security, while fast-paced and dynamic sounds can create a sense of urgency and excitement. Background music on a website or app can affect the time consumers spend on a page, as well as

their willingness to complete a purchase. In advertising campaigns, the use of specific music or sound effects can increase the effectiveness of the advertisement by creating an emotional association with the brand.

3. **Audiovisuals and Storytelling**: The use of videos in digital marketing combines visual and sound stimuli, providing a more immersive and emotional experience for the consumer. Storytelling, or narrative, is a powerful technique that uses both visual and sound stimuli to create an engaging story. By telling an emotionally engaging story, brands can establish a deep connection with consumers, increasing the likelihood of conversion. Combining a well-told story with the appropriate music and visual aesthetic can generate a strong and lasting emotional response.

These stimuli, when used strategically and consciously, not only increase the effectiveness of advertising campaigns, but also help to build a deeper and more meaningful relationship with consumers. By understanding the psychology of sensory stimuli and how they affect behavior, brands can create more impactful and effective marketing experiences, optimizing their influence on the purchasing decision process.

In short, neuromarketing is a powerful tool for understanding the subconscious processes that influence consumer decisions. By exploring brain triggers, emotions and sensory stimuli, companies can create more effective marketing campaigns tailored to consumers' emotional and psychological needs. The application of advanced technologies such as emotion tracking and brain monitoring enables a level of personalization and accuracy never before achieved, putting brands in an advantageous position to influence consumer behavior.

CHAPTER 8. ARTIFICIAL INTELLIGENCE AND ALGORITHMIC PERSUASION

Artificial intelligence (AI) has significantly transformed the way consumers interact with products and services, enabling a level of personalization never seen before. Through large-scale data analysis and the ability to learn patterns of behavior, AI systems have the power to predict users' needs before they are even explicitly expressed. This ability to anticipate and influence behavior through algorithms is known as algorithmic persuasion. In the context of marketing, AI not only recommends products based on purchase history, but also personalizes the user experience in a way that maximizes the likelihood of conversion. The use of AI to persuade users raises questions about the ethics and psychological impact of the strategies applied, especially when these approaches are imperceptible to the consumer.

How AI Anticipates and Influences Behaviors

The advancement of AI technologies has allowed companies to develop systems capable of predicting consumer behaviors with impressive accuracy. Machine learning algorithms, especially those based on deep neural networks, are trained with large volumes of behavioral data such as clicks, product interactions, and purchasing habits. These systems can identify hidden patterns in user preferences, creating detailed behavioral profiles.

This anticipation of consumer behavior can be observed in several areas, including e-commerce, streaming platforms, social networks and messaging apps. For example, on platforms like Amazon and Netflix, recommendation systems are able to suggest products or movies before the user has formulated a clear idea of what they want. This is possible thanks to a set of algorithms that analyze the user's history and the behavior of other users with similar characteristics. Furthermore, these systems are not limited to recommending what the consumer has previously purchased or watched, but also anticipate future needs, suggesting options that may not have been explored immediately.

Personalization goes beyond simply recommending products. Website and app interfaces and layouts can be adjusted according to a user's perceived preferences, making the experience more intuitive and fluid. The algorithm adjusts not only the suggestions, but also the format of the content presentation, which can include everything from the type of content to be shown to the visual style of the interface. This creates an experience that not only meets the user's expectations, but often exceeds them, without the user having to explicitly express their desires.

These AI systems, by anticipating users' actions, are able to persuade them to make decisions based on personalized suggestions. The psychological impact of this anticipation is profound: consumers begin to feel that their choices are being validated by recommendations that "know what they want", creating a feeling of control and security, but also of dependence. This perception of constant success can lead to greater loyalty to the platform or brand, as the consumer feels that the experience is shaped to meet their needs almost perfectly.

Personalized Recommendations and Their Psychological Impact

Personalized recommendations are one of the most effective forms of algorithmic persuasion, and their implementation has direct psychological implications. The psychological impact of personalization begins the moment a user realizes that a system can offer something relevant without having to explicitly ask for it. This creates a feeling of convenience and satisfaction, which can generate a strong positive association with the platform or brand. The feeling that AI "understands" the user is one of the foundations of loyalty in the modern digital world.

The psychological factor of personalized recommendations is based on the principle of *confirmation of expectations*. When an AI system suggests something that the consumer finds useful or interesting, it unconsciously validates the idea that their preferences are correctly identified. This process strengthens the bond between the consumer and the platform. The effect is even more pronounced when the recommendation is accompanied by a touch of exclusivity or rarity, such as limited discounts or exclusive products that the algorithm suggests based on user behavior.

Another important psychological aspect is the **scarcity effect**. When an AI system presents products as being "limited in stock" or "limited time on offer," it triggers fear of missing out (FOMO). This persuasion mechanism is widely used in e-commerce and can induce impulsive purchases. Artificial intelligence not only recognizes user behavior, but also adjusts the presentation of products to generate this psychological effect of urgency, motivating quick and often unplanned decisions.

AI also has the ability to adjust the pace of recommendations depending on the user's level of engagement with the platform. If a consumer constantly interacts with a specific type of content or product, the algorithm learns to provide more frequent and intense recommendations, which reinforces the habit and creates a continuous cycle of engagement. This is particularly evident on streaming platforms like YouTube and Spotify, where suggestions become progressively more aligned with user tastes and patterns, reinforcing repetitive consumption behavior.

Additionally, customization can create a **group effect**. On social media platforms, for example, AI not only analyzes individual user behavior, but also considers the behavior of other users with similar characteristics. This creates a dynamic where the consumer begins to feel part of a larger group, with preferences aligned with other people. The psychology of belonging is explored, making consumers feel more connected and, to some degree, more inclined to follow recommendations as they come with social validation from other members of that group.

The Ethics of Using AI to Persuade Users

The use of artificial intelligence to influence consumer decisions and user behavior raises complex ethical questions. As algorithms become more sophisticated, the line between providing a useful service and mishandling consumer behavior becomes increasingly blurred. Companies that use AI to personalize recommendations may be inadvertently exploiting consumers' psychological vulnerabilities, without them being fully aware of the extent to which their decisions are being shaped.

One of the main ethical concerns is the **right to privacy**. AI systems need large volumes of data to learn and make predictions about consumers. This data includes behavioral information, preferences, browsing history and even interactions on social networks. Although companies claim that this data is used to improve the user experience, the collection and use of personal information can be perceived as invasive, especially when consumers are not fully aware of how their data is being used.

Another ethical problem is the **psychological manipulation**. When an algorithm can predict and manipulate a consumer's needs and wants without them realizing it, it raises questions about consent. Algorithmic persuasion can be seen as a form of manipulation, especially if consumers are not aware of how their choices are being influenced by AI-based recommendations and stimuli. If an AI system begins to exploit emotional vulnerabilities, such as fear or the need to belong, to maximize profits, this could be considered a form of exploitation.

Furthermore, there is a risk of **manipulation of public opinion**. On digital platforms, algorithms not only personalize product and service recommendations, but also influence the way users consume information. This can affect the way people position themselves on political, social and economic issues. Algorithmic personalization can create echo chambers, where users are constantly exposed to ideas and products that reinforce their existing beliefs and preferences, rather than being challenged to explore new perspectives.

A **transparency** It is also a crucial point in the ethical debate. Because algorithms are often designed to operate in an "opaque" manner, consumers do not have a clear view of how their decisions are being shaped. Lack of transparency can generate distrust, especially when it comes to decisions involving online purchases, political choices or behavior on social networks.

Finally, it is essential that companies adopt practices **ethics** in the use of AI, respecting the limits of what is acceptable to influence human behavior. The creation of a **code of Conduct** for the use of AI in algorithmic persuasion is essential to ensure that consumers are not manipulated in unwanted ways. Transparency in data collection practices, explicit consent for the use of personal information, and accountability regarding algorithmic decisions must be fundamental pillars to ensure that AI is used ethically.

AI has significant power to anticipate and influence behavior, creating personalized experiences and persuasion strategies that are increasingly effective. Personalized recommendations, when adapted based on user behavior and preferences, have a profound psychological impact, promoting feelings of satisfaction and loyalty. However, the use of these technologies also involves ethical issues that need to be carefully considered. The manipulation of personal data, the exploitation of psychological vulnerabilities and the lack of transparency in the functioning of algorithms are risks that require strict regulation and greater awareness on the part of companies and consumers.

CHAPTER 9. THE POWER OF STORIES AND PERSUASIVE NARRATIVE

Storytelling has been a fundamental communication tool since the dawn of humanity, shaping the way individuals perceive the world around them. In the contemporary context, persuasive storytelling has been enhanced by various tools, including digital marketing strategies and social media, becoming a powerful way of influencing perceptions and decisions. In an information-saturated environment, stories have the ability to capture attention in a unique way, involving shared emotions, values and experiences. Narrative psychology, when applied to marketing and digital communication, reveals itself not only as a way of promoting products or ideas, but also as a means of shaping behavior in a subtle but highly effective way. Constructing a persuasive narrative is not just limited to verbal content, but also involves the use of images, sounds and interactivity, creating an immersive experience that stimulates emotional connection.

How Storytelling Influences Perceptions and Decisions

Persuasive storytelling has the power to alter perceptions, as it directly appeals to individuals' emotional and cognitive processes. When stories are well structured, they provide an experience that goes beyond simply transmitting information. Human psychology tends to process narratives differently than other types of content. Through emotions and plot, people are more likely to internalize the message conveyed, making it more memorable and impactful.

One of the main reasons for the power of storytelling is related to its impact on the way the human brain processes information. Studies indicate that when we are exposed to stories, our brain releases dopamine and oxytocin, chemicals that are associated with pleasure and empathy. Dopamine increases our ability to remember details, making the message transmitted more lasting. Oxytocin, in turn, creates a feeling of bonding and empathy with the characters in the story, which can be used to effectively influence perceptions and attitudes.

When telling a story, it is possible to present a sequence of events that involve challenges, overcoming and results, and human beings naturally identify with these journeys, as they are reflections of their own experiences and aspirations. This narrative format helps create a sense of progress and belonging, which can drive decisions more effectively than a simple presentation of facts.

For example, advertising campaigns that involve stories of real or fictional people in challenging situations, but with solutions offered by a particular product, are extremely effective in changing a consumer's perception of the brand or service. A good example of this is the use of customer testimonials or success stories, where the brand is positioned as the hero of the story that solves a critical problem. The empathy generated by following the character's trajectory — whether real or fictional — creates an emotional identification that leads to trust and decision-making.

The Use of Narrative Psychology in Marketing and Social Media

In the context of marketing, narrative psychology is used to deeply engage the target audience, creating an emotional experience that promotes identification with the brand, product or service. The construction of narratives within marketing campaigns is not limited to the simple display of characteristics or benefits of a product; it involves creating a story around these products, where they play a central role but are just one part of a larger plot.

Narrative psychology in marketing uses a series of psychological and behavioral elements to maximize the impact of the message. One of these elements is the **character creation** that consumers can identify with. These characters do not have to be real people, but can be symbolic representations of an ideal consumer type or a specific target audience. The central character can be an individual who faces a common problem and finds a solution through the use of the product or service, which creates an immediate emotional connection with the audience.

Another important component is the **use of emotions**. Emotionally charged storytelling tends to be more effective at capturing attention and eliciting a response. If a story appeals to emotions such as happiness, sadness, fear or surprise, it tends to generate greater engagement. Intense emotions activate areas of the brain that are responsible for forming lasting memories, increasing the chance that the consumer will remember the product or service when making future decisions.

In the age of social media, persuasive storytelling is amplified by the ability to create a continuous, interactive narrative. Platforms like Instagram, Facebook, Twitter and TikTok allow brands to connect with consumers on a more personal level, using a combination of text, image, video and interactivity. The narrative, in this case, is not just consumed passively, but becomes a collaborative experience, where followers can engage, react and even influence the course of the story.

A classic example of storytelling marketing on social media is **#LikeAGirl campaign**, from the Always brand. Rather than simply selling a product, the brand created a narrative about women's self-esteem, challenging the negative stereotypes associated with doing things "like a girl." This campaign generated strong engagement while promoting the product in a way that aligned with the target audience's values and concerns.

The use of **influencers** It is also an important storytelling strategy on social media. Brands often partner with influencers who share their own stories or product experiences, creating an authentic narrative that resonates with their followers. The influencer's personal story becomes part of the persuasive narrative, with the brand as a facilitator of this positive experience.

Examples of Storytelling Applied to Digital Persuasion

Storytelling applied to digital persuasion involves more than simply telling a story; it's about structuring that story strategically to maximize the emotional impact and, eventually, conversion of a target audience. Next, we will see some practical examples of how storytelling can be effectively applied to digital persuasion.

1. **Advertising Video Campaigns**: Video campaigns are one of the most effective forms of storytelling in digital marketing. A good example of this are the advertising campaigns created for Christmas, where brands develop stories that touch on themes such as family, generosity and togetherness. By using visual and emotional storytelling, these campaigns connect directly to the audience's values and feelings, creating a positive association with the brand.

   A company like Coca-Cola, for example, by creating Christmas campaigns with stories about the spirit of generosity, is able to associate its products with the emotional experience of the season, generating a bond with consumers. By doing this, the brand is not just promoting soft drinks, but creating a narrative that associates the consumption of the product with special, familiar and positive moments, which makes consumers choose the brand as part of their celebrations.

2. **Storytelling em E-commerce**: In the context of e-commerce, storytelling can be used very effectively to increase the conversion rate. For example, rather than simply showcasing a product, an e-commerce site might include a story about how the product was developed,

how it solves a common problem, or how it has a positive impact on consumers' lives. A sportswear company, for example, can tell the story of an athlete who overcame great challenges, and how using the brand's products was fundamental to his journey.

3. **Content Marketing and Blogs**: Content marketing also benefits enormously from storytelling. Brands create blogs that not only provide information about their products, but also include stories about how their products have impacted consumers' lives. For example, a cosmetics brand might share the story of a customer who used one of their products and experienced a significant transformation in her confidence or self-esteem. These stories generate an emotional connection with the audience and make the product more desirable.

4. **Interactive Experience in Digital Marketing**: In some cases, digital storytelling becomes interactive, creating an immersive experience that allows consumers to participate in the narrative. Platforms like games and augmented reality experiences are ideal for this. Cosmetics brands, for example, can use augmented reality to allow consumers to virtually try on different products and share their transformation "stories" on social media. These types of experiences help create a stronger emotional connection with the brand, making consumers feel part of the narrative.

5. **Influencers and Customer Testimonials**: Storytelling is also reflected in the use of digital influencers and customer testimonials. When an influencer shares a personal story about how a certain product or service made a difference in their life, they use storytelling to build an emotional bond with their followers. By adopting storytelling in an authentic and relevant way, influencers create content that resonates with their followers, helping to persuade and motivate purchasing decisions.

Persuasive storytelling is one of the most powerful tools in the digital marketing arsenal. By building engaging and emotional stories, brands can not only capture consumers' attention, but also shape their perceptions and influence their decisions in profound ways. Narrative psychology allows brands to connect with consumers on an emotional level, creating a lasting association between the product and the audience's values or needs. The strategic use of storytelling on social media and in marketing campaigns has proven increasingly effective in a digital environment saturated with information. By adopting these techniques, companies not only sell products, but create experiences that resonate emotionally with their consumers, driving loyalty and, consequently, sales.

CHAPTER 10. GAMIFICATION AND REINFORCEMENT PSYCHOLOGY

Gamification is a concept that has become popular in several areas, from digital marketing to education and the healthcare sector. The fundamental principle of gamification is the use of game elements and mechanics, such as rewards, challenges and points systems, to encourage engagement and shape behaviors in ways that would be more difficult to achieve through traditional methods. The psychological impact of gamification is profound, and its use in areas such as education, healthcare and commerce has shown significant results, not only in terms of engagement, but also in terms of motivation, learning and even changing habits. This chapter will explore how games and reward systems shape behaviors, how challenges and achievements can be used to increase engagement, and the psychological impact of gamification in these different industries.

How Games and Reward Systems Shape Behavior

The psychology behind gamification is deeply rooted in the principles of reinforcement and motivation. Games, at their core, are built to maximize intrinsic and extrinsic motivation. Intrinsic motivation is that which comes from within the individual, such as the pleasure or personal satisfaction of carrying out a task or achieving a goal. Extrinsic motivation refers to external rewards, such as prizes or recognition, that encourage behavior.

In games, these two types of motivation are often combined. The search for rewards, such as points, medals or new skills, serves as an extrinsic incentive, while the experience of completing challenges and advancing in the game can be motivated by internal satisfaction. Reinforcement psychology, which is based on the idea that behaviors can be modified and maintained through rewards and punishments, plays a fundamental role in this process.

Games use a concept called **variable reinforcement**. Instead of rewarding the player after every action (continuous reinforcement), the reward system is structured in an unpredictable way, which keeps the player engaged for longer. This type of reinforcement is highly effective because it creates a sense of anticipation and excitement. The player never knows when the next reward will come, which makes them keep playing, waiting for the next achievement.

This type of reinforcement is widely used in gambling and online games, where the reward can be something as simple as a score or as complex as a rare item. The psychology behind this is that the uncertainty of when the reward will occur keeps players motivated. This same approach can be applied outside of games, such as in company loyalty programs or wellness apps.

A **Deci and Ryan's theory of human motivation**, which includes the self-determination model, is also relevant here. This model suggests that people have three basic psychological needs: competence, autonomy, and relatedness. In a game, players may feel that they are growing in skill (competence), that they have control over their choices (autonomy), and that they are connected to a community of other players (relationships). These factors, when well balanced, not only encourage engagement, but can also generate a deep sense of satisfaction and accomplishment.

Using Challenges, Achievements, and Levels to Increase Engagement

Games are famous for their ability to create engaging challenges that keep players engaged for long periods of time. Creating progressive challenges, which become more difficult as the player progresses, is one of the main reasons games are able to maintain an active and engaged user base. In a gamification context, challenges are created to engage users so that they feel they are moving towards a goal, whether tangible, such as a prize, or intangible, such as a sense of personal accomplishment.

The concept of **difficulty levels** is one of the simplest yet effective ways to increase engagement. In games, players start with easy tasks, and as they become more skilled, the tasks become more difficult. This gradual increase in challenge keeps players interested as they feel like they are being challenged in a way that aligns with their skills. When applying gamification to other areas, such as education or corporate training, challenges can be structured in a similar way, creating a learning curve that maintains engagement.

The introduction of **achievements** it is also a central aspect of gamification. Achievements are milestones that players reach after reaching certain goals, such as completing a mission or reaching a score. In the context of gamification in work or educational environments, achievements can be used to reward student or employee progress, encouraging them to continue striving. Achievements can take many forms, such as badges, medals, or certificates, and are often accompanied by ranking systems, which encourage healthy competition among participants.

These reward and recognition systems are powerful because they not only reward effort but also provide constant feedback. Immediate feedback is a crucial element in reinforcement psychology. It helps individuals understand which behaviors are being rewarded and which are not. This constant feedback strengthens motivation and engagement, creating a cycle of encouragement.

The Psychological Impact of Gamification in Education, Health and Commerce

The application of gamification in different sectors has proven effective in shaping behaviors, improving information retention, promoting healthy habits and increasing user engagement.

Next, we'll explore how gamification has impacted education, healthcare, and commerce.

Education: Gamification has been widely applied in education, where it has become an effective tool for increasing student engagement and improving learning outcomes. Instead of simply conveying information, educators can incorporate game elements such as points, levels, and achievements to make learning more interactive and engaging. Gamification systems on online learning platforms such as Khan Academy and Duolingo are good examples of how this can be done.

These platforms encourage students to advance in their studies by rewarding them with points or badges each time they complete a module or achieve a specific objective. This approach not only keeps students engaged, but also creates a sense of progression and accomplishment. Additionally, gamified activities can be structured to meet individual learning needs, allowing students to progress at their own pace, which is key to intrinsic motivation.

A **healthy competition** also plays an important role. On many educational platforms, students can compare their performance with others, which creates an environment of friendly competition that can motivate students to improve. However, it is important that this competition is balanced, so that it does not become excessively stressful or demotivating for students.

Health: In the healthcare sector, gamification has been successfully used to promote healthy habits, such as physical exercise, balanced eating and adherence to medical treatments. Health apps like Fitbit and MyFitnessPal incorporate gamification elements, rewarding users for reaching physical activity goals or logging their meals. These rewards can include points, badges or even competitions between friends.

Gamification has also been applied in software programs **rehabilitation** and **psychological treatment**, where progress is rewarded with achievements that reflect the patient's effort. This type of reward system is particularly effective for individuals who struggle with motivation to adhere to exercise regimens or follow treatment plans. The use of gamification elements helps transform these often arduous processes into something more enjoyable and engaging.

Business: In commerce, gamification has been an effective tool for increasing customer loyalty and improving the shopping experience. Gamified loyalty programs, where customers earn points or rewards for their purchases, have proven effective in encouraging repeat purchases and brand engagement. Brands like Starbucks and Sephora use points systems that reward consumers for their purchases and interactions with the brand.

Furthermore, gamification is also used on e-commerce platforms to encourage purchasing behavior, through elements such as progressive discounts, shopping challenges or rewards for completing certain actions, such as sharing products on social media or writing product reviews.

The psychological impact of gamification in commerce is great, as it not only encourages repeat purchasing, but also creates a sense of belonging and reward that keeps customers coming back.

Gamification, when applied correctly, can shape behaviors in powerful and effective ways. Reinforcement psychology is a key driver of this transformation, using progressive rewards, feedback and challenges to increase engagement and encourage action. Whether in education, healthcare or commerce, gamification has proven to be a valuable tool for improving user experience, encouraging learning, promoting healthy habits and increasing customer loyalty. By understanding the psychological principles that underpin gamification, it is possible to create more effective systems that meet individuals' needs, keeping them motivated and engaged in the long term.

CHAPTER 11. SOCIAL MEDIA PERSUASION: THE MASS EFFECT

The influence of social media on contemporary society is undeniable. They have become not only platforms for social interaction, but also powerful tools of persuasion, capable of shaping behaviors, decisions and attitudes. Persuasion on social media goes beyond simple marketing strategies; it involves a set of psychological elements that direct users to act in certain ways, often without realizing how much they are being influenced. Collective behavior, driven by **social proof**, for the **power of digital influencers** and by **viralization of content**, is the basis of many phenomena that occur on social networks. This chapter addresses these aspects and how they affect individuals' decision-making and the psychological impact generated by this process.

How Social Proof Influences Decision Making

A **social proof** is a fundamental psychological principle that refers to the tendency of individuals to copy the actions of others, assuming that these actions reflect correct behavior. This concept has its roots in social psychology, particularly in the work of **Robert Cialdini**, which explored how people make decisions based on observing others, especially in situations of uncertainty. On social media, this phenomenon is amplified, as users are often exposed to the choices and behaviors of a large number of people. Social proof manifests itself in many forms, such as comments, ratings, number of likes, shares, and even the popularity of certain influencers or brands.

When a product, service or idea receives many likes or shares, it signals to other users that this choice is valid or desirable. This effect is especially strong when we observe that people with whom we have some degree of identification or admiration are adopting a certain action. For example, a post with thousands of likes can create a feeling that it is worthy of attention, influencing the behavior of users who have not yet decided whether or not to interact with that content.

On a deeper level, social proof also manifests itself in environments where mass behavior appears to be the **social norm**, becoming almost an unspoken rule of compliance. Platforms like **Instagram**, **TikTok** and **Facebook** operate within this concept, where content that is widely engaged (commented on, shared, liked) is often prioritized by the algorithms of these networks, creating a **popularity spiral** which can generate more engagement simply because it is already popular.

This phenomenon can be viewed in terms of positive feedback. When users see that something is widely accepted or appreciated, they tend to associate that content with high value, whether in the informative, social or entertainment aspect. This is effective in several areas, such as digital marketing, where brands exploit this principle by encouraging customers to leave positive reviews about their products or services. These testimonies form a **social proof** that influences other consumers to make similar choices.

Digital Influencers and the Power of Mass Persuasion

You **digital influencers** play a central role in the social media ecosystem, using their **perceived authority** and **capital social** to impact the decision-making of its audiences. Influencers' persuasion goes beyond simple product promotion; it involves a complex process of building trust, authenticity and emotional connection with your followers. Influencers are not just celebrities or famous people; they can be any individual with a significant and engaged audience on a given social network. Their power comes from their ability to generate **credibility** and **personal relationship** with your followers.

The relationship between influencers and their followers is mediated by **psychology of affect** and **of identification**. When a follower begins to identify with an influencer, they tend to trust that influencer's recommendations more immediately, often without questioning the authenticity or motivation behind the choices made. This identification is often cultivated through regular interactions and the sharing of similar personal experiences and values.

The persuasive power of influencers is amplified by the fact that they function as a **extent of social proof**. When an influencer promotes a product or behavior, he validates this choice, making his followers perceive the action as something desirable or even necessary. This is because, in many cases, the relationship between influencer and follower becomes **emotional**, and the follower feels that the influencer's choice is an extension of their own identity.

Furthermore, the **anchoring effect** is often used by influencers when highlighting specific products or services as "favorites" or "essentials." By establishing these items as points of reference, influencers anchor the decisions of their followers, who begin to consider them more valuable compared to other options available on the market.

This dynamic is particularly relevant in **affiliate marketing**, where influencers earn commissions for promoting products. In this context, influencers not only share their personal experiences with products, but also create a sense of urgency or **exclusivity**, often using phrases like "limited stock" or "exclusive offer." This tactic activates the **fear of losing** (FOMO), making followers feel like they need to act quickly to avoid missing a unique opportunity.

The Viralization of Content and Its Psychological Impacts

A **viralization of content** is another central phenomenon in social media and is closely linked to mass persuasion. When content goes viral, it reaches a significantly greater number of people in a short period of time, often beyond the content creator's initial control. This type of dissemination can occur due to a combination of factors, such as relevance, timing, emotional appeal or, more frequently, the content's ability to resonate. **connect with the values or feelings of the masses**.

The psychology behind going viral involves the concept of **emotionality**. Content that evokes strong emotions – whether positive or negative – tends to be shared more. THE **emotional contagion effect** is the phenomenon in which one person's emotions influence the emotions of another, which is enhanced on social media. When content provokes laughter, anger, surprise or sadness, it creates a strong desire to share it with others in order to generate the same reaction in other users.

Viralization is also fueled by the idea of **tribalism**. When content spreads, it usually does so because it resonates with specific groups of people, who identify with the message or idea expressed. This type of content can be something that reinforces shared beliefs or behaviors, such as social movements, cultural trends, or even memes. Identification with a group and the desire to **belong** are powerful motivators of action. Going viral not only occurs because the content is widely shared, but also because it activates the social networks of a cohesive group of individuals who, in turn, share the content with their own networks, creating a multiplier effect.

The psychological impact of going viral is significant. Firstly, it can increase the perception of **social validity**. The more people share or interact with content, the more legitimate it appears. This creates a cycle of validation where an individual's behavior (sharing, liking, commenting) is influenced by the interaction of others.

Furthermore, viralization can cause a **disinhibition effect**. Anonymity or the feeling of being in a mass network can make people feel freer to express opinions, behaviors or reactions they normally wouldn't have. This can be observed in phenomena of **aggressive comments**, **public controversies** and even in campaigns **disinformation**. The psychological impact here is twofold: on the one hand, going viral offers a sense of belonging and validation, but on the other hand, it can lead to a **polarization** or **extremization** of opinions.

Finally, viralization can also have **negatives** on the mental health of individuals. THE **social comparison effect** it is exacerbated when observing viral content, especially when this content shows standards of life, success or happiness that seem unattainable. Constant exposure to this type of content can generate feelings of inadequacy, anxiety or depression, especially among young people.

Persuasion on social media is not just a matter of influencing individuals to make decisions, but also of understanding the psychological mechanisms that govern those choices. Social proof, the power of digital influencers and the virality of content are powerful forces that shape the way people interact with the digital world and make decisions in their everyday lives. By understanding these dynamics, it is possible to not only harness the principles of persuasion for business or marketing purposes, but also gain critical insight into how these influences shape society more broadly.

CHAPTER 12. THE EFFECT OF COLORS, SOUNDS AND SHAPES ON PERSUASION

Persuasion is not limited to textual or verbal messages; it also involves visual and sound elements that have significant power over individuals' emotions and decisions. Colors, sounds and shapes can have subtle but profound influences on the way we perceive our environment and make decisions. On digital platforms, the strategic application of these elements is one of the most effective tools for directing user behavior and ensuring they take specific actions. This chapter addresses how visual and sound elements affect individuals' emotions and decisions, exploring the effects of typography and color on digital platforms and analyzing case studies on the strategic use of design to influence users.

How Visual and Sound Elements Affect Emotions and Decisions

Visual and sound design has the ability to change the perception of a brand, product or service. These elements can evoke emotions, which in turn influence purchasing decisions, engagement and loyalty. Psychologists and designers have long studied how different visual characteristics, such as colors, shapes, patterns, and the arrangement of elements on a page or interface, affect user behavior.

You **visual elements** are often the first thing a user notices about an interface, and the initial perception can determine whether or not the user decides to interact with the content. Colors, typography and the general structure of a layout are able to communicate implicit messages, which can be interpreted differently depending on the experiences, cultures and emotional states of those who observe them. Colors, for example, can induce feelings of calm, urgency or excitement, influencing decision-making in powerful ways.

You **sound elements** play an equally important role. Sounds and music can create a sense of urgency, joy, or suspense depending on how they are used. On many digital platforms, such as websites, games or apps, background music and sound effects can make a huge difference to the way a user feels when browsing. Using appropriate sounds can also enhance the immersive experience and facilitate decision-making, encouraging action.

Colors and their Associated Emotions

Colors have a profound psychological effect. Each color can evoke a specific range of emotions, which are widely recognized and used in design and marketing strategies. For example:

- **Red:** It is an energizing and stimulating color, often associated with passion, urgency and excitement. It is commonly used in calls to action, such as purchase buttons, promotions or alerts. It can increase time pressure and induce quick decisions.
- **Blue:** It evokes feelings of calm, confidence and professionalism. It is often used by companies seeking to convey stability and security. Banking or investment platforms generally use blue to convey trust and credibility.
- **Yellow:** Associated with energy, joy and optimism, yellow is used to attract attention and create a welcoming environment. However, excessive use can be perceived as tiring.
- **Green:** This color is often associated with health, tranquility and nature. It conveys a feeling of balance and harmony, being used by brands that want to convey well-being or sustainability.
- **Therefore:** Black can be elegant, sophisticated and mysterious. It is used by premium or luxury brands, as it conveys a feeling of exclusivity and high quality.

- **Orange:** Orange is vibrant and stimulating, associated with creativity and energy. It is often used to attract attention in a less aggressive way than red, and is also effective in calls to action.
- **White:** White represents simplicity, purity and clarity. Often used in minimalist designs, white can create a clean and organized environment, promoting legibility and facilitating navigation.

These color associations are strategically exploited to influence user behavior. A page's design, for example, can be optimized to generate an emotional response that encourages the desired action. If the goal is to create a sense of urgency, like in a limited-time promotion, using red can be effective. If the objective is to convey trust and stability, especially in financial services, blue is the most suitable color.

The Impact of Typography and Colors on Digital Platforms

On digital platforms, the combination of colors and typography has a significant impact on the user experience and their decision to continue browsing or make a purchase. THE **typography**, together with the colors, creates a cohesive visual identity and makes the content easier to read and understand.

The use of **typography** It's key to establishing information hierarchy and ensuring users can navigate pages without feeling overwhelmed. The choice of font, size and spacing between characters are crucial decisions to ensure fluid and comfortable reading. Sans serif font types such as **Helvetica** and **Arial**, are commonly used in digital interfaces because they are more readable on screens. On the other hand, serif fonts like **Times New Roman**, are associated with a more formal and traditional aesthetic.

The choice of typography must also be aligned with the brand's personality. For example, if the brand is young and dynamic, you can use modern, stylized typography. A brand that values tradition and seriousness can opt for more classic and structured fonts.

Furthermore, the **typography color** is also important. Black text is the most readable, but it can be interesting to use alternative colors to highlight important elements, such as calls to action or titles. Contrasting colors, such as white text on a dark background, are also effective for creating an impactful visual, but you need to balance the use of colors to avoid compromising readability.

On e-commerce platforms, for example, it is common to see a combination of **buttons in vibrant colors** (like red or orange) with **clear and direct typography** that instructs the user what to do, such as "Buy Now" or "Learn More." These visual elements are carefully chosen to maximize conversions and ensure the user takes the desired action.

Case Studies on the Strategic Use of Design to Influence Users

1. **Amazon and the Urgency in Shopping** Amazon is a clear example of how design can be used to generate urgency and encourage purchases. The platform uses color **orange** on action buttons like "Add to Cart" and "Buy Now". This color, in addition to attracting attention, is associated with energy and action, encouraging users to make quick decisions. The use of **simple and direct typography**, such as "Free Shipping" and "Fast Delivery", also creates a sense of urgency while communicating an immediate benefit, making the purchasing decision easier.

2. **Airbnb and Trust in the Reservation Process** Airbnb uses **blue** as one of the predominant colors in its design, conveying confidence and security. This is especially important on platforms that deal with financial transactions and long-term bookings. Choosing simple and elegant fonts like **San Francisco** and **Helvetica Neue**, helps create fluid, frictionless navigation, promoting confidence in the booking experience. The company also uses **high quality photographs**

to showcase accommodations, creating an emotional connection with users and encouraging the choice of a specific property.

3. **Spotify and the Personalization of User Experience** Spotify is an example of how sounds can be used strategically to create a personalized and immersive experience. The platform uses **personalized songs and playlists** based on user behavior and preferences. Furthermore, the **dark color palette** with **vibrant details** helps maintain attention on the content and creates a sense of immersion, allowing users to focus on the listening experience. The combination of sounds and colors in its design conveys a feeling of exclusivity and personalization, encouraging users to explore the platform further.

4. **Apple and Minimalist Design** Apple is a classic example of effective, minimalist design. The brand uses **the white** as the predominant color in its design, creating a feeling of clarity and simplicity. The typography used is always clean and easy to read, reinforcing the idea of sophistication and modernity. By creating an intuitive interface without information overload, Apple is able to capture users' attention and encourage purchasing decisions in a subtle way, without forcing consumer behavior.

Persuasion through visual and sound elements is one of the most powerful strategies used on digital platforms. The combination of colors, typography and shapes can evoke emotions that directly influence users' decisions. When these elements are applied strategically, they can create an engaging and targeted user experience, encouraging specific actions such as purchasing, engaging or joining a platform. Designers and marketers must understand the emotions and psychographic responses associated with each visual and sound element so they can create effective interfaces and campaigns that positively impact user behavior.

CHAPTER 13. CONSUMER PSYCHOLOGY AND ONLINE SHOPPER BEHAVIOR

Consumer purchasing behavior is increasingly influenced by a series of psychological factors, from emotions to heuristics that shape the way decisions are made. In a world where digital commerce dominates, understanding the psychology behind these decisions is essential to creating effective marketing strategies, optimizing the user experience and increasing conversion rates. This chapter explores how emotions and heuristics affect digital shopping, the role of mental triggers in marketing strategies, and the psychological factors that influence customer loyalty.

How Emotions and Heuristics Affect Digital Shopping

Emotions play a central role in the purchasing decision process. Unlike pure logic, which could guide a purchase just by analyzing features and prices, emotions often act as a catalyst for the final decision. In the digital environment, where the consumer does not have a tactile experience of the product, emotions can be even more amplified.

Heuristics They are mental shortcuts that people use to make decisions quickly. They function as general rules or "tricks" that help the brain save time and energy when processing information. When it comes to online shopping, consumers often apply heuristics such as "if it's popular, it must be good", or "if the price is high, it must be good quality". These simple rules help shoppers make decisions in a shopping environment saturated with options, but often these heuristics can be manipulated to increase sales.

For example, the use of **scarcity** or **urgency** can mislead consumers into believing that a product is highly desired, or that they must act quickly to take advantage of a unique opportunity. This type of tactic exploits the fear of missing an opportunity (FOMO - Fear of Missing Out), a powerful emotion that can lead to impulsive decisions.

Furthermore, the **heuristic analysis** also applies to price perception. When a consumer sees a 50% discount on a product, the brain may immediately associate it with a great deal without considering the real factors justifying the original price. This heuristic is effective because it appeals to humans' natural desire to take advantage of a "good" opportunity, even if this is not always rational.

Emotions such as happiness, fear, anxiety or pleasure are deeply rooted in online purchasing decisions. When a consumer visits a website and comes across a product that evokes positive emotions, such as nostalgia, or that solves an immediate problem, they may be led to make a purchasing decision without weighing all the pros and cons. The emotions associated with the product can create a bond, making the purchase more attractive. You **anchoring effects** are also powerful, where a higher price first, followed by an offer or discount, can make the original price seem more justifiable, changing the perception of the product's value.

The Use of Mental Triggers in Marketing Strategies

Mental triggers are powerful tools that marketers use to influence consumer decisions. They work on a subconscious level, activating automatic responses and triggering emotional reactions that can encourage consumers to take action.

Scarcity is one of the most effective mental triggers. E-commerce sites often display messages such as "only 3 units left" or "offer valid until midnight", creating a sense of urgency that drives the consumer to act before the opportunity disappears. This trigger uses the **psychology of fear of missing out** to motivate purchase. The idea that something could disappear quickly triggers a primal impulse to action, forcing the consumer to make a quick decision.

Another powerful trigger is the **commitment and consistency**. When a consumer commits to a small action, such as filling out a registration form or adding an item to their cart, they feel obligated to follow through with the purchase. This initial commitment triggers the need to maintain consistency, leading the consumer to take the final action, which is purchase. Once the individual has invested a little time or effort, he tends to complete the action to justify that small initial investment.

The trigger of **authority** is also widely used. When a product is recommended by an authority figure or a recognized brand, consumers tend to trust the quality and value of the product more. Using expert or influencer testimonials can create a sense of trust, encouraging the consumer to make a decision based on the **social proof**. A **social proof** is another mental trigger that is fundamental in marketing strategies. If a consumer sees that other people are buying or recommending a product, they tend to follow the crowd. This behavior is ingrained in our social nature: if lots of people are doing something, it seems like the right choice. This can be seen in product reviews, the number of likes on a post, or the number of shares of a promotion.

A **reciprocity** is another trigger that acts on consumer psychology. When a brand offers something of value to the consumer, such as a discount, exclusive content or a free sample, the individual feels the need to return this favor, often with a purchase. This exchange creates a feeling of debt, which is a powerful motivator of actions, including in digital commerce.

The reciprocity can be applied to tactics such as offering a **discount coupon** for new customers or allow them to try a service for a free trial. This gesture creates an emotional relationship, where the consumer feels they need to reciprocate, often through a purchase.

Psychological Factors that Affect Customer Loyalty

Customer loyalty is one of the biggest challenges and, at the same time, one of the biggest objectives of companies in the digital environment. Retaining a customer and ensuring they come back for more purchases involves a deep understanding of the psychological factors that influence ongoing consumer behavior.

The trust is the first and most important factor. Consumers must feel that the brand is trustworthy before they make a purchase and, more importantly, before they become loyal customers. To build this trust, brands must ensure a consistent, flawless experience. This includes having a **responsive website**, easy to navigate, with **clear information** about the product, terms of service and return policies. Transparency in transactions, including security in payment processing and protection of personal data, is also fundamental to creating a relationship of trust.

A **customization** is another important psychological factor that affects loyalty. When a consumer feels treated uniquely, their loyalty tends to grow. This can be achieved through targeted marketing campaigns, recommendations based on past purchases or browsing behaviors, and personalized product offers. Brands must use available data to create a more personalized shopping experience, creating an emotional bond with the customer.

A **customer satisfaction** is a crucial factor in ensuring that he becomes loyal to the brand. The customer experience, from the moment of purchase to after-sales, must be positive and exceed expectations. The way a company handles problems, such as returns or complaints, also impacts loyalty. Resolving a problem quickly and effectively creates a positive perception, even in situations that may have initially been frustrating for the customer.

THE **continuous engagement** It is also an important psychological factor in loyalty. By maintaining contact with consumers after the sale, whether through email marketing, newsletters or personalized notifications, companies keep their brand present in the consumer's mind. Offering relevant content such as blogs, videos or webinars can increase perceived brand value and create an ongoing relationship.

A **exclusivity** is another factor that can increase loyalty. Offering exclusive benefits like early access to product launches, member discounts, or exclusive events creates a sense of belonging and reward. This makes the customer feel special and more likely to continue purchasing from the brand.

Online buyer behavior is strongly influenced by psychological factors involving emotions, heuristics and mental triggers. Smart use of these elements can optimize marketing strategies and increase conversion rates, encouraging consumers to make quick, impulsive decisions. At the same time, understanding how trust, personalization and customer satisfaction affect loyalty can help brands build lasting relationships with their consumers. Through consumer psychology, companies can not only sell products, but create experiences that turn consumers into loyal brand advocates.

CHAPTER 14. PERSUASION AND FAKE NEWS: HOW PEOPLE ARE MANIPULATED

The spread of fake news is one of the biggest challenges of the 21st century, especially with regard to the impact it has on people's decisions and social behavior. With increasing dependence on the internet as the main source of information, many people are exposed to a variety of content that is not always truthful. In an information-saturated environment, fake news spreads quickly, often influencing attitudes, beliefs and actions in significant ways. To understand how this happens, it is necessary to explore the concepts of persuasion, confirmation bias, the role of algorithms and the psychological strategies that contribute to the creation and propagation of persuasive narratives.

Confirmation Bias and Its Relationship to Misinformation

Confirmation bias is a psychological phenomenon where people tend to seek, interpret and remember information in a way that confirms their pre-existing beliefs or hypotheses. This bias is not just a cognitive flaw; it is deeply rooted in human nature and influences the way information is processed and accepted. When applied to news consumption, confirmation bias can help explain why fake news is so effective at shaping opinions and spreading misinformation.

When a person encounters news or information that reinforces what they already believe, they tend to accept it without question. This happens because, cognitively, it is easier and more comfortable to accept information that validates our beliefs than to confront it with new data that could destabilize our worldview.

On digital platforms, where information is often filtered by algorithms, individuals end up consuming content that aligns with their perspectives, amplifying their beliefs and making it more difficult to access alternative views.

Fake news takes advantage of this bias by presenting information that is emotionally attractive or confirms preconceived ideas. For example, a person who already has a negative view of a certain politician may be more receptive to fake news that describes that politician in a harmful way, without verifying the veracity of the information. In many cases, confirmation bias creates a bubble of misinformation, where individuals continue to be fed narratives that reinforce their view, with no room for questioning or considering other points of view.

Furthermore, confirmation bias is also present in the choice of information sources. Many people prefer to consume content from sources that share their political, religious or ideological beliefs, which creates a cycle where fake news can be disseminated without any opposition. This effect is magnified in online communities, where people often cluster around similar interests and beliefs, making them more susceptible to manipulative messages.

The Role of Algorithms in the Spread of Fake News

The algorithms that govern social media platforms and search engines play a fundamental role in the spread of fake news. These algorithms are designed to maximize engagement, meaning they prioritize content that generates the most reactions, such as likes, shares, and comments. Unfortunately, fake news is often more emotional and controversial, which makes people engage with it more intensely, causing this content to be promoted by algorithms.

When a person interacts with fake news, whether sharing it, commenting or just liking it, the algorithm interprets this action as a sign that the content is relevant and displays it to more people. This cycle of positive engagement creates an environment where fake news can spread quickly, without any type of veracity verification. The algorithm does not have the ability to distinguish between true and false information; it only assesses the level of engagement, and fake news, as it is often more sensationalist or polarizing, is more likely to generate reactions.

In many cases, algorithms also create filter bubbles, where users are exposed to information that confirms their preexisting beliefs and interests. This happens because algorithms tend to show users content similar to what they have already consumed, creating a network of information that reinforces each person's worldviews. This personalization, although it offers convenience, also facilitates the spread of fake news, as people are not confronted with different perspectives or sources of information that could question the veracity of the content they are consuming.

Furthermore, the fragmentation of information on social networks also facilitates the spread of fake news. Unlike traditional sources of information, such as newspapers and magazines, which have an editorial structure and fact-checking processes, digital platforms allow anyone to publish and share information without any type of supervision. This creates a space where fake news can spread without any control or accountability.

The use of bots and fake accounts also contributes to the problem. Bots are programmed to disseminate content in an automated manner, often further expanding the spread of fake news. They can create the impression that information is more popular or accepted than it actually is, which can induce others to accept it as true. When this information spreads quickly and reaches large audiences, it can be seen as more credible, even if it is unsubstantiated.

Psychological Strategies Used to Create Persuasive Narratives

Fake news and manipulative narratives often use a series of

psychological strategies to make their messages more persuasive. These strategies exploit cognitive flaws and human emotions to trick people into believing something without questioning or investigating the veracity of the information. Here are some of the key techniques used to create persuasive narratives.

1. Emotional appeal: Many fake news appeal to the most basic human emotions, such as fear, anger, disgust or sadness. This is because people tend to process emotional information more quickly and with greater intensity than rational information. Narratives that provoke these emotions tend to be more effective, as people are not thinking logically, but reacting instinctively. For example, fake news about an imminent danger can generate panic, leading people to share it without checking its veracity.

2. Oversimplification: Fake news often oversimplifies complex issues, presenting a distorted or oversimplified version of an event or idea. By reducing a complex problem to a simple, clear narrative, fake news becomes easier to understand and more convincing. This technique is effective because people tend to prefer simple explanations over more detailed or complicated information.

3. Appeal to authority: Fake news often uses seemingly credible sources to reinforce its message. This could include experts, public figures, or organizations that appear trustworthy but are actually promoting misinformation. By citing authorities or experts, even in a manipulative way, fake news gains legitimacy and becomes more difficult to question.

4. Repetition: The more information is repeated, the greater the chance of it being accepted as true. This technique, known as the **effect of repetition**, is widely used in the propagation of fake news. People tend to believe information more when it is repeated frequently, even if it is incorrect. This can be seen in disinformation campaigns, where a false message is repeated in various media, creating the impression that it is true.

5. False equivalences: Another common trick in fake news is to create false equivalences, where information from different sources is treated as if it carries the same weight, even when one source is clearly more reliable than the other. By equating sources of information without considering their credibility, fake news manipulates public perception, making it more difficult to distinguish between what is true and what is not.

6. "Us versus them" narratives: Many fake news create a confrontational narrative, dividing people into opposing groups. This can be seen in political campaigns, where fake news paints one side as the hero and the other as the villain. This type of narrative exploits social polarization, encouraging hostility and misinformation, and makes people accept a distorted version of reality, without considering the nuances and complexities of a situation.

7. Appeal to scarcity and urgency: Fake news often includes a sense of urgency or scarcity to prompt people to act quickly. This can be seen in messages that warn of an imminent threat or an opportunity for action that is about to disappear. Time pressure creates an emotional pull, causing people to engage without thinking critically about the information.

The manipulation of information through fake news is a growing threat, driven by cognitive biases, social media algorithms and well-designed psychological strategies. Confirmation bias, for example, causes people to seek information that confirms their preexisting beliefs, making them more susceptible to misinformation. Furthermore, digital platform algorithms amplify the spread of fake news by prioritizing content that generates high engagement, regardless of its veracity. Fake news uses a series of psychological strategies to become more persuasive, such as emotional appeals, oversimplification and repetition. Understanding these dynamics is essential to develop strategies to resist misinformation and promote a more critical and responsible consumption of information.

CHAPTER 15. PSYCHOLOGY OF FEAR AND URGENCY IN THE DIGITAL ENVIRONMENT

The psychology of fear and urgency has been widely explored in the digital environment, especially in online marketing and security. Both emotions, when applied well, have the power to influence users' decision-making in a significant way. In the digital context, fear can be used to create a feeling of threat or risk, while urgency drives people to act quickly, without time to consider options. Both strategies have been successfully applied to manipulate behaviors, from product consumption to the adoption of digital security practices. Next, we discuss the ways in which fear and scarcity are used in different online contexts, the techniques that make use of these elements and the impacts they have on users' decisions.

How Fear and Scarcity Are Used to Generate Immediate Action

Fear and scarcity are two of the most powerful psychological triggers in persuasion. They are used to speed up decision making by encouraging users to act without prolonged reflection. Fear can be an effective tool when there is a perceived threat that requires an immediate response, while scarcity uses the idea of limited availability to create momentum for action.

Fear as a Trigger for Immediate Action

Fear has a profound impact on human decisions. In the digital context, fear is often used to induce a sense of urgency or panic, leading users to take impulsive actions. Marketing campaigns, cybersecurity alerts, and even political messages can strategically use fear to generate immediate response.

In marketing, a classic example of the use of fear is the "fear of missing out" strategy (FOMO – Fear of Missing Out). This technique is used in limited sales advertisements, where the user is informed that a product is about to sell out or that a promotion is about to end. The feeling that something good might be lost creates an impulse to buy immediately, without the need for additional consideration. Scarcity, as an element combined with fear, makes the product or offer more attractive.

In the context of digital security, "security at risk" warnings often exploit fear by informing users about the possibility of data theft, viruses or online fraud. These alerts often exaggerate the risk, making the user feel that immediate action is necessary to avoid harm. For example, a notification about a potential phishing attack may be accompanied by urgent instructions to change passwords or install a security update. The fear of suffering catastrophic consequences such as data loss or unauthorized access leads users to make quick decisions such as clicking links or making changes without fully questioning the situation.

Scarcity as an Urgency Trigger

Scarcity is another psychological principle often explored in the digital environment. The idea that a feature or offering is limited in quantity or time can prompt users to act quickly. Scarcity doesn't have to be real to be effective; Simply suggesting that an item or opportunity is about to disappear can have a huge impact on consumer behavior.

In digital marketing, the concept of scarcity is widely used in sales and promotion campaigns. A common example is the use of countdown timers, where consumers see a countdown of time until a special offer or discount expires. This type of technique creates a sense of urgency and pressures users to make quick decisions. Scarcity is also applied in "limited stock" or "last units available" advertisements. Even though the product is still widely available, this information makes consumers feel like they need to act quickly or they will miss the opportunity.

Scarcity is also used on social media platforms, where the idea of "limited time" is often associated with posts, offers or products. Special promotions for a limited number of users or exclusive benefits for those who act quickly can encourage a sense of urgency to interact with content or make a purchasing decision.

Techniques Used in Marketing and Digital Security to Influence Users

Digital marketing and online security are increasingly intertwined in their approaches to persuasion, using the same techniques to influence users. In both areas, psychological persuasion strategies are used to attract attention, incite fear, and encourage immediate action. The following techniques are some of the most used:

1. Time Urgency and Limited Offers

One of the most common techniques is creating a sense of urgency through countdown timers and limited offers. "Last 24 hours" or "only 10 spots left" offers are typical examples of this strategy. It appeals to the fear of missing an opportunity, making the user feel that if they don't act quickly, they will miss something important. These offers are often accompanied by messages such as "don't miss this unique opportunity" or "grab now before it's too late".

2. "Immediate Danger" and "Action Required" Announcements

In the context of digital security, users often receive messages like "Your computer is at risk!" or "Security alert! Update now!". These messages trigger an emotional response of fear and urgency. The goal is to make the user feel that immediate action is necessary to avoid larger problems. Often, these messages are not as dramatic as they seem, but are phrased to make an immediate emotional impact.

3. Appeals to Exclusivity

Exclusivity is another common technique, both in marketing and digital security. In marketing, exclusive products or offers like "members only" or "early access for you" create a sense of belonging and value. This appeal to exclusivity makes the user feel privileged, which leads them to act more quickly.

In the context of digital security, appeals to exclusivity can be seen in phishing or scam alerts, where a user may be informed that they are one of the "select few" to receive a special security warning or an exclusive upgrade offer. This creates a sense of privilege and urgency.

4. Security and Protection Guarantees

In many cases, companies use fear of risk to generate trust. This is widely used in digital security, where users are prompted to purchase antivirus or protection software when alerted to imminent threats. Ads like "Protect your privacy now" or "Prevent data loss with our solution" are common. These messages appeal to the need for security and protection against invisible threats, generating an emotional response from the user.

5. Challenges and Pop-up Notifications

A technique used in both marketing and digital security is the use of pop-ups or notifications that demand an immediate response. These notifications are often designed to appear to require urgent action, such as "Click here to continue" or "Action required to avoid risk." This type of approach creates an artificial sense of urgency and pressures users to make quick decisions, whether to buy something, update software or click on a link.

The Impact of Fear on Online Decision Making

Fear, when applied strategically, can have a profound impact on the way people make decisions online. This impact is often amplified by the impulsive nature of digital interaction, where decisions are made quickly, often with little thought.

The fear of missing an opportunity or suffering immediate harm can lead users to act impulsively. This can result in decisions that, under normal circumstances, would be more considered. For example, a person may end up purchasing a product or service without proper research, simply for fear of missing out on the offer. In a similar way, users may be tricked into clicking links, installing software, or sharing personal information without considering the risks involved, all because of the fear of not acting in time.

Fear can also distort the perception of risks. When bombarded with alarming information, such as advertisements about "hackers breaking into systems" or "online fraud on the rise," users may end up exaggerating their threat perception, leading them to take hasty actions that may not be necessary or beneficial. Additionally, fear can cause people to underestimate or ignore greater risks, focusing only on immediate, visible risks.

Ultimately, fear and urgency are two of the most powerful forces in the psychology of the digital environment. These emotions can be manipulated to generate quick responses and impulsive decisions, from purchasing products to installing security updates. By understanding how these techniques work and how they affect online behavior, users can become more critical and aware of persuasion strategies that attempt to influence their decisions.

CHAPTER 16. PERSUASION IN DIGITAL HEALTH AND WELLBEING

Digital persuasion has gained significant relevance in the most varied fields, and the area of health and well-being is no exception. By applying psychological principles and behavioral strategies, it is possible to induce users to adopt healthy habits, both in relation to physical and mental health. However, with increasing dependence on digital technologies, new risks arise, such as digital overexposure and behavioral burnout. The use of persuasive technologies to promote healthy lifestyle habits must be done carefully, considering both the benefits and negative impacts that digitalization can bring to well-being.

Applications of Digital Persuasion in the Adoption of Healthy Habits

Digital persuasion can be used effectively to encourage the adoption of healthy habits, whether through apps, wearable devices or online health platforms. These tools often use elements of behavioral psychology, such as rewards, positive feedback, and gamification, to engage users and encourage them to achieve health-related goals.

Persuasion in Promoting Physical Activity Habits

One of the most evident examples of the use of digital persuasion is to encourage physical exercise. Fitness apps, such as Strava, Nike Training Club, and Fitbit, integrate persuasive techniques to motivate users to achieve physical activity goals. Persuasion strategies range from using daily notifications reminding the user to move, to implementing challenges and competitions with friends or other platform users.

These apps use the concept of variable rewards, which is a positive reinforcement technique based on behavioral psychology. Each time the user reaches an activity goal, they receive a reward, which can be a virtual badge, an achievement or even a digital certificate. This reward creates a feeling of satisfaction and motivation, encouraging the user to continue with the desired behavior. At the same time, daily notifications act as constant reminders, activating the user's conditioned response and making exercise an increasingly automatic routine.

Feedback and Monitoring Techniques

Another important aspect of digital persuasion on health habits is feedback. Many health apps provide immediate feedback on the user's performance, whether in terms of the number of steps taken, the number of calories burned or the time spent physical activity. This feedback is crucial to keeping the user engaged and helping them see the progress they are making.

Feedback can also be configured to highlight success. When the user achieves a goal or performs a health-related task, such as drinking the recommended amount of water or getting enough sleep, they receive motivational messages. This type of digital persuasion creates a sense of accomplishment, reinforcing positive behavior and encouraging the continuation of healthy habits.

Personalization and Relevance

Personalization is another key factor in digital persuasion, especially in healthcare apps. By collecting data on users' habits and behaviors, these applications are able to personalize recommendations for physical activity, nutrition and even mental health monitoring. Personalization makes suggestions more relevant to the user, increasing the chances of adherence to suggested habits.

In many cases, personalization also involves adapting goals according to the user's skill level or activity history. For example, if a user is just starting to exercise, the app could suggest more modest goals, such as walking for 10 minutes a day, and gradually increase as the user progresses. This prevents overload and ensures goals are challenging but achievable.

Persuasive Technologies in Mental and Physical Health Applications

In addition to physical health apps, mental health apps also make extensive use of digital persuasion to promote psychological well-being. The difference here is that, rather than focusing on physical behavior, persuasive technologies are used to engage users in improving mental health, whether through meditation, cognitive behavioral therapy (CBT) or mood monitoring.

Meditation and Relaxation Apps

Apps like Calm, Headspace, and Insight Timer apply persuasive techniques to help users incorporate meditation practices into their daily routine. These platforms use a combination of motivational elements such as rewards (medals and badges), positive feedback and timers to create a sense of progression and encouragement.

These apps also make use of daily notifications, such as reminders to meditate or tips for practicing breathing techniques. By implementing this approach, apps ensure that meditation becomes a regular part of the user's day, creating a positive habit loop. Additionally, many of these platforms offer structured meditation programs that start with short sessions and gradually increase in time, which makes it easier for the user to adapt and maintain engagement.

Digital Cognitive-Behavioral Therapy (CBT)

On another note, mental health apps like Woebot and Youper use elements of Cognitive Behavioral Therapy (CBT) to help users deal with issues such as anxiety and depression. These apps are designed to provide therapy in a digital format using interactive chats where users can talk to a virtual assistant. Persuasion here occurs through constant interaction and continuous feedback about the user's feelings and thoughts.

Digital persuasion in these cases is based on the idea that user behavior can be modified with regular, personalized intervention. By tracking the user's emotional state and suggesting activities to improve well-being, such as breathing techniques, reevaluating negative thoughts or simple relaxation exercises, the app becomes a continuous support tool for mental health.

Mental Health Monitoring and Gamification

Just like physical health, gamification also plays an important role in mental health. Apps like Moodfit and Sanvello use games and points systems to keep users involved in the mental health care process. Additionally, these apps often integrate mood tracking, allowing users to record how they feel over time.

These gamification practices create a fun approach to keeping users motivated to engage in self-discovery and emotional care activities. Seeing the results of your progress — such as increasing points or unlocking new levels of emotional skills — makes the experience more rewarding and encourages continued use of the app.

The Risk of Digital Overexposure and Behavioral Burnout

While persuasive technologies bring clear benefits to adopting healthy habits, there is a dark side to overreliance on digital tools to improve well-being. The risk of digital overexposure is a growing reality, where the continuous use of devices and applications can lead to mental and emotional exhaustion. Digital burnout is a phenomenon that occurs when the user feels overwhelmed by the amount of information, tasks and expectations imposed by digital platforms.

The Impact of Digital Burnout on Mental Health

Digital burnout is characterized by feelings of fatigue, anxiety and a feeling of being constantly "connected" or "available", which can be harmful to mental health. Constantly monitoring health-related data such as weight, number of steps or stress levels can create pressure to achieve unrealistic goals. This incessant monitoring can transform the process of taking care of your health into a strenuous task, generating an effect opposite to that desired.

Furthermore, overexposure to health and well-being notifications can create a feeling of constant urgency, which, instead of encouraging the practice of healthy habits, generates anxiety. In many cases, users feel pressured to achieve quick results or follow an excessive number of wellness programs, which can lead to a state of emotional exhaustion.

Strategies to Avoid Digital Burnout

To mitigate the risk of digital burnout, it is essential that developers of healthcare apps and platforms create systems that respect user limits. Introducing "rest" features, where the user can set time limits for using the app, or "breaks", where the app suggests rest periods between sessions, can help reduce pressure.

Furthermore, personalizing goals and adapting the digital experience according to the user's progress are also important strategies. The emphasis should not only be on the amount of activities performed, but also on the balance and general well-being of the user.

Digital persuasion plays a significant role in promoting healthy habits, both in terms of physical and mental health. Through technologies such as fitness, meditation and therapy apps, it is possible to positively influence users' behaviors, encouraging them to adopt healthier habits. However, it is critical that developers of persuasive technologies consider the risk of digital overexposure and burnout by creating platforms that not only engage users but also promote a healthy balance between technology and well-being.

CHAPTER 17. DIGITAL EDUCATION AND THE USE OF PERSUASION FOR ENGAGEMENT

Digital education has become an integral part of the modern educational landscape, transforming the way people learn, engage with content and develop skills. Applying persuasive techniques in the educational context is a powerful tool for increasing engagement, improving knowledge retention, and encouraging positive behaviors in the learning environment. These techniques, often used on online educational platforms, can be employed to motivate students, keep them focused, and ensure they achieve their educational goals.

By approaching the psychology of learning and the persuasion techniques used on educational platforms, it is possible to understand how digital environments shape the learning experience. Furthermore, personalizing educational content has been shown to be an effective approach to increasing engagement, making the learning experience more relevant and motivating for students.

How Educational Platforms Use Persuasive Techniques

Educational platforms, whether aimed at teaching technical skills, academic courses or corporate training, employ a series of persuasive techniques to maximize user engagement. These techniques are based on behavioral psychology and instructional design principles, aiming to create more engaging and effective learning experiences.

Gamification and Rewards

Gamification is one of the main persuasive techniques used on educational platforms. Incorporating game elements, such as points, badges, leaderboards and virtual rewards, transforms the learning process into a more fun and competitive experience. This type of extrinsic motivation creates an environment where students are constantly challenged to achieve new things, which can increase engagement and content retention.

For example, platforms like Duolingo, which teaches languages, use points, badges and daily challenges to keep students motivated. With each lesson completed, users earn points and can see their progress on a leaderboard. This not only motivates students to continue studying, but also creates a sense of accomplishment when goals are achieved.

The key to the success of gamification on educational platforms lies in the application of variable rewards, a concept derived from behavioral psychology. When the reward is not given in a predictable way, students tend to become more involved in the process, as uncertainty about the reward makes the behavior more rewarding. This type of reinforcement, when combined with clear objectives, helps increase students' intrinsic motivation.

Immediate Feedback

Immediate feedback is another crucial persuasive technique in digital learning. By providing instant feedback on students' actions, educational platforms help reinforce correct behavior and quickly correct mistakes. This type of feedback can be implemented in several ways, such as automatic assessments, correction of responses in real time, or even suggestions for improvements based on the student's performance.

Immediate feedback has a direct impact on knowledge retention as it allows students to quickly know what they are doing right and what they need to improve. On platforms like Coursera and Khan Academy, for example, students receive feedback on the tests and exercises they take, allowing a clearer understanding of their progress and identifying areas where they need to focus more.

Social Reinforcement

Using social reinforcement is a powerful technique that involves creating a sense of community and connection among students. This can be done in a variety of ways, such as discussion forums, study groups, team challenges, and real-time interactions with instructors. Educational platforms often encourage collaboration among students, which can increase engagement with content and improve learning outcomes.

By allowing students to share their achievements, compare their progress with others, and engage with peers, platforms create an environment where learning becomes a social experience. Social reinforcement, especially on platforms like edX and Udemy, can be a great motivator as learners feel supported and encouraged by other members of the learning community.

Content Personalization

Personalizing educational content is one of the most effective ways to increase engagement and knowledge retention. When students have the ability to adapt their learning according to their needs, interests and abilities, the learning process becomes more relevant and meaningful. Personalization can come in many forms, such as adapting the pace of learning, selecting specific topics of interest, or providing personalized support resources.

Platforms like Khan Academy and edX use algorithms to adapt content based on student performance. If a student demonstrates a deeper understanding of a topic, the system can offer more difficult challenges, while if the student struggles, the content will be revised or explained in a simpler way. This type of personalization creates an environment where students feel more in control of their learning, which can increase motivation and reduce frustration.

The Psychology of Learning and Knowledge Retention

The psychology of learning is essential to understanding how persuasive techniques can be used to improve the educational experience. The learning process involves the acquisition, retention and application of knowledge, and educational platforms can greatly benefit from applying psychological principles to optimize each of these phases.

The Forgetting Curve

The forgetting curve, proposed by Hermann Ebbinghaus, suggests that people tend to forget a large amount of information soon after learning it, especially if there is no reinforcement or review. To combat this phenomenon, educational platforms use spaced repetition techniques, where content is reviewed at increasingly longer intervals. This helps reinforce knowledge and ensure it is retained for a longer period of time.

Platforms like Anki, a flashcard system, apply the spaced repetition technique in an automated way, providing review cards at the moment when the student is about to forget the information. This significantly increases learning efficiency and helps keep knowledge stored in long-term memory.

The Self-Determination Theory

Self-determination theory, proposed by Edward Deci and Richard Ryan, suggests that intrinsic motivation is more effective for long-term learning than extrinsic motivation. This means that students are more likely to learn effectively when they are genuinely interested in the content and have control over how, when and what they learn. To foster intrinsic motivation, educational platforms must create an environment that offers autonomy, competence and relationships.

Personalizing content and being able to choose your learning pace and methods are effective ways to promote self-determination. Additionally, positive feedback and a sense of constant progress also help increase feelings of competence, which strengthens intrinsic motivation.

Active Learning

Active learning is an approach that emphasizes student involvement in the learning process rather than simply receiving information passively. Active learning techniques such as quizzes, practice exercises, and group discussions are widely used on educational platforms to encourage students to engage with content in a meaningful way.

By incorporating active learning, educational platforms create opportunities for students to reflect on what they have learned, apply knowledge to real-world situations, and discuss concepts with peers. This not only improves content comprehension but also facilitates long-term retention.

The Impact of Personalization on Educational Engagement

Personalization has a significant impact on educational engagement by tailoring the learning experience to individual students' needs and preferences. When content is personalized, students feel more connected to the material and are more likely to engage in the learning process.

Adaptive Learning

Adaptive learning is one of the most advanced forms of personalization in the educational field. It uses algorithms to automatically adjust content based on student performance. This means that as the student progresses, the system can increase the difficulty or provide additional supporting materials depending on the student's needs.

Platforms like Duolingo, Khan Academy and Smart Sparrow implement adaptive learning systems, allowing content to adjust in real time to student responses and performance. This creates a more fluid and personalized learning experience where students can progress efficiently, at their own pace, without feeling overwhelmed or unmotivated.

The Importance of Relevance

In addition to adjusting content difficulty, personalization also involves making content more relevant to learners. By understanding students' preferences, interests, and goals, platforms can provide resources and activities that are more aligned with what each student finds most interesting or important.

For example, if a student is studying for a specific exam or trying to develop a skill for a career, the platform can tailor content to meet those goals. This increases engagement as students see the direct value in what they are learning and how it can benefit them in the long run.

Persuasive techniques play a crucial role in increasing educational engagement by helping students stay motivated, focused and committed to the learning process. Educational platforms that utilize gamification, immediate feedback, social reinforcement, and content personalization are more effective in creating engaging and impactful learning experiences. Additionally, understanding the psychology of learning and applying theories such as the forgetting curve, self-determination, and active learning can significantly improve knowledge retention.

As digital education continues to evolve, the use of persuasive techniques and content personalization will become even more sophisticated, providing students with a highly effective, motivating and personalized learning experience. Educational platforms that adopt these approaches will have a positive impact on creating more capable individuals who are better prepared to face the challenges of the future.

CHAPTER 18. ETHICS AND TRANSPARENCY IN THE PSYCHOLOGY OF DIGITAL PERSUASION

The use of persuasion psychology in the digital environment has expanded exponentially, with online platforms, applications and services adopting techniques to influence user behavior. Digital persuasion is a valid practice when applied ethically, respecting users' rights and promoting positive experiences interacting with technology. However, the line between persuasion and manipulation is fine, and transparency in the application of these techniques is essential to ensure that users do not fall victim to unfair or harmful practices. To ensure that the use of digital persuasion is ethical, it is necessary to understand the line between persuasion and manipulation, the role of privacy and informed consent, and the responsible practices that platforms should adopt when applying such techniques.

The Limit Between Persuasion and Manipulation

Persuasion and manipulation can be difficult to distinguish, as they both involve the use of psychological techniques to influence behavior. However, the crucial difference lies in the intention and transparency of the process. Persuasion is a legitimate practice when it aims to positively and respectfully influence individuals' decisions, leading them to make choices that benefit both them and the platform. On the other hand, manipulation aims to deceive or coerce individuals into making decisions that harm them, often without their full consent or understanding.

Ethical Persuasion

Ethical persuasion seeks to align user needs with the platform's intentions. When a platform uses persuasion techniques such as content personalization, gamification or real-time feedback, the goal should be to help users achieve their goals more effectively and satisfactorily. For example, a language learning app might use rewards and challenges to encourage students to continue their lessons, but the intention is to ensure that the student benefits from the content and progresses in their learning. This results in a win-win situation, where the user feels motivated and the platform achieves its engagement goals.

Ethical persuasion must be transparent. Users must be fully aware of the persuasive techniques being applied. This means that, for example, if a service is collecting behavioral data to personalize the user experience, the platform must be clear about what is being collected, how it will be used, and what benefits it will bring to the user.

Manipulation and Its Effects

Digital manipulation is characterized by the unfair use of psychological techniques, with the aim of deceiving or coercing users into making decisions that are not in their best interests. Manipulation can manifest itself in several ways, such as the use of false urgency tactics, where users are pressured to make quick decisions without adequate reflection, or the use of "dark pattern" techniques, where interfaces are designed in a way that deceives users or makes it difficult to make informed decisions.

For example, when creating an online shopping website, a platform may use a dark default, such as the "opt-in" option to sign up for promotional emails, which is predefined, causing the user to sign up without realizing it. Or, you can create a sense of urgency, such as displaying a countdown timer indicating that an offer is about to expire, even when the promotion is valid for longer. These practices not only violate users' trust, but can also have long-term negative effects on the relationship between the platform and the user.

Manipulation is harmful to users as they are being influenced in a way that is not fully transparent and is often contrary to their own interests. This leads to a loss of trust and can result in damage to the reputation of the platform adopting such practices.

The Role of Privacy and Informed Consent

Privacy and informed consent are fundamental pillars of any ethical digital interaction. As digital platforms become more sophisticated in their data collection and application of persuasive techniques, ensuring that users understand how their information is being used and that they have control over this is essential to maintaining an environment of respect and trust.

Privacy in the Digital Context

In an increasingly digitized world, user data has become a valuable resource. Platforms and companies collect large volumes of data about users' behaviors, preferences and interactions with the aim of personalizing the experience, increasing engagement and driving sales. However, user data must be treated with maximum respect and protection.

Privacy in the digital context involves ensuring that users have full control over the information they share. Platforms must be clear about what data they are collecting, how that data will be used, who will have access to it, and how long it will be stored. An example of this can be seen on social media platforms, which must provide easy and accessible options for users to manage their privacy settings and choose how their data is used.

Furthermore, there must be a limitation on the type of data collected. Excessive information collection can be seen as a violation of privacy, especially when the data collected is not necessary for the user experience. Platforms must be transparent about the data they collect and ensure that this data is only used for the purposes for which it was collected.

Informed Consent

Informed consent is a legal and ethical principle that requires users to fully understand the implications of their actions before agreeing to something. In the digital context, this means that platforms must provide clear and understandable information about how user data will be collected, used and shared, and users must have the choice to consent or not to this.

Informed consent must be expressed actively, that is, the user must take the initiative to accept or reject privacy policies and terms of service. This consent should not be assumed by default, and users should have the ability to revoke their consent at any time without hassle. A common approach to this is the use of consent pop-ups or banners that clearly explain the terms and give the user the option to accept or decline data collection.

In some regions, such as the European Union, the General Data Protection Regulation (GDPR) sets out clear rules on how consent must be obtained and platforms' obligations regarding data privacy. GDPR requires platforms to provide specific, detailed consent and to respect users' right to access, correct or delete their personal data.

Responsible Practices for Using Digital Persuasion

While digital persuasion techniques can be effective in improving user engagement and experience, they must be used responsibly and with respect for the rights of individuals. There are several responsible practices that platforms can adopt to ensure that digital persuasion does not turn into manipulation.

Transparency and Clarity

One of the main responsible practices is transparency. Platforms must be clear about the persuasion techniques they are using and how these practices benefit users. This includes clearly explaining how content is personalized based on users' actions and behaviors, how algorithms are used to suggest products or content, and how rewards are applied in the gamification process.

Additionally, platforms should avoid using manipulative tactics that could mislead users or trick them into making decisions without fully understanding the consequences. This includes eliminating dark patterns and applying design practices that promote informed and autonomous choices.

Strengthen Active Consent

Another responsible practice is to reinforce users' active consent. Platforms must obtain clear and explicit permission from users before collecting their data or applying persuasive techniques such as content personalization. This must be done on an ongoing basis, allowing users to update their preferences or withdraw their consent whenever they wish.

Prioritize User Well-Being

Platforms must adopt a user-centric approach, prioritizing user well-being and experience in all their persuasion practices. This means that, rather than just seeking to maximize screen time or engagement, platforms must consider the impact of their actions on users' mental health, free time and digital-life balance.

Ethics and transparency in the use of digital persuasion psychology are fundamental to ensuring that platforms promote a positive and respectful experience for users. By adopting responsible practices, platforms can influence user behavior in ways that benefit everyone, without resorting to manipulation or deception. Privacy and informed consent are pillars of this ethical approach, allowing users to have control over their information and choices. By following these guidelines, educational platforms and other digital services can create experiences that not only increase engagement but also promote trust and mutual respect between the parties involved.

CHAPTER 19. HOW TO PROTECT YOURSELF FROM UNWANTED PERSUASION

In the digital environment, we are constantly exposed to persuasive techniques that seek to shape our behavior and influence our decisions. From personalized advertising to algorithm-based notifications and suggestions, digital persuasion is present in almost every online interaction. While many of these techniques are designed to improve the user experience and help you find what you want, they can also be used in manipulative ways, directing individuals' choices without their full consent or understanding.

To protect yourself from unwanted persuasion, it is crucial to understand the techniques used, recognize the cognitive biases that influence our decisions and adopt practices that preserve autonomy in online choices. This chapter covers how to increase awareness of persuasive techniques, how to avoid cognitive biases and digital pitfalls, and the tools and practices available to ensure you have control over your digital decisions.

Strategies for Raising Awareness of Persuasive Techniques

The first step to protecting yourself from unwanted persuasion is to increase awareness of the techniques used by digital platforms. Tech companies have access to vast amounts of data about our online behaviors and use this knowledge to create highly personalized experiences and influence our decisions. These techniques are often invisible to users, making it difficult to identify when they are being manipulated.

One of the most effective ways to raise awareness is to educate yourself about how algorithms work. Digital platforms, such as social networks and e-commerce sites, use algorithms to recommend content, products and services based on the user's previous behavior. These algorithms are designed to maximize engagement, often leading users to make decisions they wouldn't have made if they had a full, informed view of the options available.

Additionally, it is important to understand the design patterns that can be used to manipulate choices. "Dark patterns" are a technique often used to trick users into making decisions they don't want to make, such as subscribing to newsletters without their explicit consent or making it difficult to delete an account. Knowing these techniques helps you identify when a platform is using these methods and make more informed decisions about how to interact with it.

Another crucial point to increase awareness is transparency on the part of platforms. While many digital platforms use persuasion techniques, few provide clear information about how and why users are being influenced. Companies must adopt transparent practices, allowing users to know how their data is being used, what persuasion techniques are being applied and the impact of this on their choices.

How to Avoid Cognitive Biases and Digital Traps

Cognitive biases are systematic distortions in thinking that can affect the way we make decisions. These distortions are widely exploited by digital platforms to influence users' choices. By understanding how cognitive biases work, we can take steps to avoid them and thus maintain control over our decisions.

Confirmation Bias

Confirmation bias occurs when we look for or interpret information in a way that confirms our preexisting beliefs or opinions, while ignoring information that might contradict them. Digital platforms, especially social networks, exploit this bias, offering content that reinforces users' beliefs and opinions. This creates a filter bubble, where users are only exposed to information that aligns with their worldview, making them more susceptible to manipulation.

To avoid confirmation bias, it's important to actively seek out information that challenges our beliefs and exposes us to different points of view. Additionally, it's helpful to use navigation tools that provide a variety of information sources, rather than relying on a single personalized feed.

Anchoring Effect

The anchoring effect is a cognitive bias in which a person gives excessive weight to the first information received, even if it is irrelevant or misleading. For example, when seeing an original price of R$1,000.00 and a discount to R$500.00, the consumer may be led to believe that they are getting a good deal, even if the value of R$500.00 is still higher than the market value for the product.

E-commerce platforms often utilize this bias, showing high original prices and significant discounts, creating a sense of urgency to make a decision. To avoid this bias, it is important to stop and critically evaluate the proposal before acting, always trying to compare prices and understand the real value of what is being offered.

Scarcity Bias

Scarcity bias occurs when we perceive something as more valuable or desirable because of its limited availability. Digital platforms often use this bias, showing messages such as "last units", "limited promotion" or "exclusive offer", inducing users to make quick decisions without fully considering the consequences.

While scarcity bias can be effective in increasing sales or engagement, it can also lead to hasty decision-making. To avoid this bias, it is important to adopt a more reflective approach and avoid acting on impulse when faced with an offer that appears to be in short supply. Asking yourself if you really need the product or service and considering other options can help you make more rational decisions.

Deserving Effect

The deservingness effect is a cognitive bias in which people tend to believe that they deserve something simply because they are being presented with an offer or reward. This is often exploited in loyalty programs, where users feel like they should take advantage of an offer because they "deserve" a reward or bonus, even if it's not something they really want or need.

To avoid this bias, it is essential to question whether the offer or reward really has value for you or whether it is being imposed by the platform. Instead of accepting a reward immediately, reflect on your real need and the impact of the decision.

Tools and Practices to Maintain Autonomy in Online Decisions

In addition to increasing awareness of persuasive techniques and avoiding cognitive biases, there are several tools and practices that users can adopt to ensure their online decisions are informed and autonomous.

Privacy Settings and Data Control

One of the simplest ways to maintain control over online decisions is to adjust privacy settings on digital platforms. Social networks, for example, offer settings that allow users to limit who can see their posts, personal data and activities. By reviewing and customizing these settings, users can reduce the amount of data collected and used to personalize their experience.

Additionally, many platforms now offer tools to visualize and control how your data is used. For example, on Google, you can go to the "My Activity" section to review collected data, such as searches and ad interactions, and adjust your ad preferences. By using these tools, users can make more informed decisions about what they share and how their information is used.

Privacy-Focused Browsers

Another important practice is the use of privacy-focused browsers, such as Tor or Brave, which help protect personal data and reduce the collection of information by advertising platforms. These browsers block trackers and cookies, making it difficult to collect data about a user's browsing habits. By using these tools, you can reduce your exposure to personalized ads and other forms of digital persuasion.

Disable Notifications and Alerts

Many digital platforms, such as social networks and shopping apps, send notifications to encourage users to return to the service and interact with it. These notifications can be persuasive, creating a sense of urgency and forcing quick decisions. To avoid this pressure, turning off unnecessary notifications can help you stay focused and avoid unwanted distractions. By turning off notifications, users can make more deliberate and less impulsive decisions.

Use of Extensions and Plugins

There are several browser extensions and plugins that help protect users from unwanted persuasion. Tools like "uBlock Origin" and "Privacy Badger" block ads and trackers, while others like "Dark Patterns" and "TrackThis" warn about the use of manipulation techniques on websites. These extensions help users maintain control over their online experience and avoid digital pitfalls.

Digital persuasion can be a powerful tool for improving the online experience, but it can also be used in manipulative and harmful ways. To protect ourselves from unwanted persuasion, it is essential to raise awareness about the techniques used, understand how cognitive biases influence our decisions, and adopt practices that help us maintain autonomy in our digital choices. With the appropriate tools and strategies, it is possible to browse the internet in a more informed and conscious way, ensuring that our decisions are based on our own needs and not on external influences.

CHAPTER 20. THE FUTURE OF DIGITAL PERSUASION

Digital persuasion is constantly evolving, following the technological innovations that emerge and modify the digital landscape. Emerging technologies, such as artificial intelligence, augmented reality, neural interfaces and new ways of interacting with platforms, bring both new opportunities and challenges for individuals seeking to preserve their autonomy in decision-making. The future of digital persuasion inevitably involves a greater degree of sophistication in the techniques used to influence users and, at the same time, an increasing need for individuals to understand and protect themselves from these influences.

Furthermore, new media and neural interfaces not only make digital interactions more immersive, but also more powerful in the way they can shape people's emotions and behaviors. How can we deal with these new challenges? And how can we develop a more conscious and ethical relationship with technology, which allows us to enjoy its benefits without being dominated by its persuasive strategies?

Emerging Technologies and New Challenges for Digital Persuasion

With the continuous advancement of technologies such as artificial intelligence, machine learning and big data, digital platforms have access to more information about users than ever before. This has enabled unprecedented personalization of digital experiences. Through highly sophisticated algorithms, platforms know what you like, who you interact with, which products or content you are most likely to consume, and even the patterns of your emotional behavior. This results in a much more targeted and, consequently, more persuasive user experience.

However, the use of personal data by these platforms also raises ethical questions about privacy and control over the information itself. Although technology companies have access to these vast amounts of data, many users are not fully aware of the extent to which their information is being used to influence their choices. With this comes the challenge of ensuring that persuasion techniques do not exceed the limits of ethics, creating a fine line between the benefit of a personalized experience and the deliberate manipulation of user behavior.

Artificial intelligence, for example, is capable of analyzing behavior patterns more accurately and efficiently than any human being. It can be used to predict how a user will react to an advertisement, a product recommendation or even a social interaction within a social network. These predictions can be extremely effective, but they can also be used to manipulate users in ways they don't realize, creating a vicious cycle where people's decisions are constantly shaped without them realizing how much they are being influenced.

The Impact of New Media and Neural Interfaces on Human Influence

New media, which include platforms such as virtual reality (VR) and augmented reality (AR), are transforming the way we interact with technology. These media offer a much more immersive and sensorial experience than traditional computer screens or smartphones. By combining digital elements with the real world, AR and VR interfaces are able to create environments and experiences that completely capture the user's attention, making them more vulnerable to persuasive influences.

On an augmented reality platform, for example, you may be presented with ads and product recommendations that are integrated into your physical environment, creating an experience that feels more personal and relevant. These experiences can be so realistic and engaging that people can make decisions based on them without realizing they are being persuaded.

Furthermore, neural interfaces, which include technologies such as implantable chips and wearable devices that can interact directly with the human brain, promise to open a new chapter in interaction with technology. While these technologies are still in their early stages, they have the potential to profoundly change the way we process information, interact with devices, and make decisions. With the ability to capture neural signals directly from the brain, companies can not only understand our deepest intentions, but also influence our cognitive and emotional responses much more effectively.

The use of neural interfaces can also introduce a new dimension of persuasion, as devices will be able to access real-time data about users' mental and emotional states. This could allow, for example, a system to automatically adjust the content shown to maximize the user's emotional response, creating an even more persuasive and immersive consumer experience.

The ethical challenge that arises with these new technologies is how to ensure that they are used responsibly without compromising the autonomy of individuals. While digital persuasion technologies already offer a significant degree of personalization, neural interfaces and augmented reality further expand the possibility of influencing people's decisions and behaviors, raising questions about consent, control and privacy.

How We Can Develop a More Conscious Relationship with Technology

As digital persuasion technologies become more sophisticated and immersive, the need to develop a more conscious relationship with technology becomes even more urgent. Digital awareness is critical to ensuring that individuals can make informed choices and maintain their autonomy, even in a highly persuasive digital environment.

One way to cultivate this awareness is to educate yourself about digital persuasion techniques and how they affect our decisions. This includes learning to identify "dark patterns" – those designs and practices that aim to trick users into making decisions they wouldn't normally make. With this knowledge, users can become more vigilant regarding the products and services they consume online, making decisions based on critical analysis rather than an automatic response to persuasive stimuli.

The second important strategy is implementing digital mindfulness practices. Mindfulness refers to the practice of being aware and present in the moment, without being dominated by automatic thoughts or emotions. By applying this practice to our use of technology, we can become more aware of the automatic impulses and reactions that occur as we interact with digital platforms. This can help reduce the influence of persuasive techniques that seek to manipulate our decisions. A simple way to apply digital mindfulness is to take moments to disconnect from technology, reflect on the choices made online and assess whether they really meet our needs or whether they were influenced by persuasive strategies.

Furthermore, it is essential to support the implementation of regulations and public policies that protect users against data misuse and manipulative techniques. Governments and international organizations need to work to establish standards that ensure technology companies operate ethically and transparently, respecting the privacy of individuals and ensuring that their decisions are not unduly influenced.

Another crucial aspect of a more conscious relationship with technology is the promotion of digital literacy. This involves teaching people to use technology critically and reflectively so they can identify persuasion techniques and resist them when necessary. Digital literacy must be taught from basic education so that individuals grow up with the skills necessary to consciously navigate the digital world.

Ethics in technology design also plays an important role in this process. Technology companies need to adopt responsible design practices, taking into account the psychological and emotional impacts of their platforms on users. This means that when creating products and services, companies must be transparent about how their algorithms work, ensure users can easily control privacy settings, and offer clear and fair choices without using manipulative techniques.

The future of digital persuasion is closely linked to the advancement of emerging technologies, which bring both challenges and opportunities. New media, such as augmented and virtual reality, and neural interfaces, have the potential to make digital persuasion even more powerful and immersive, but they also raise significant ethical questions about privacy, consent, and control. To address these challenges, it is essential to cultivate a more conscious and ethical relationship with technology, which includes education about persuasion techniques, implementing digital mindfulness practices, supporting the ethical regulation of technology, and promoting digital literacy.

As these technologies continue to evolve, the key to ensuring they benefit society in a fair and balanced way will be the ability of individuals to maintain their autonomy and make informed choices, even in an increasingly persuasive digital environment.

FINAL CONCLUSION

Throughout this book, we explore the fascinating and complex intersection between psychology and digital persuasion. Communication technologies and digital platforms have radically transformed the way we relate to the world around us, directly influencing our decisions, behaviors and perceptions. From the first chapters, we seek to understand how the foundations of the psychology of persuasion were applied to the digital environment, to the ethical and social implications that arise as technology advances. This book not only offers a deep insight into how persuasive techniques operate, but also proposes a critical reflection on the challenges we face as a connected society.

Chapter Summary

Chapter 1: Fundamentals of the Psychology of Persuasion The first chapter lays a solid foundation, presenting the fundamental principles of classic persuasion and its evolution in the digital context. Persuasion, at its core, involves changing attitudes, beliefs or behaviors, and throughout history, psychologists like Aristotle and Freud helped shape the practices that would eventually be adapted for digital environments. With the advent of communication technologies, persuasion has become more systematic and measurable, being amplified by algorithms and digital marketing techniques.

Chapter 2: Psychological Models Applied to Digital Persuasion In this chapter, we delve deeper into the psychological models that are crucial to understanding digital persuasion. We highlight the Cialdini Model, with its six principles of influence – reciprocity, commitment, consensus, authority, scarcity and sympathy. We also discuss the Fogg Model, which explores the intersection between human behavior and technology, as well as other approaches that help explain how users interact with digital platforms.

Chapter 3: The Impact of Personalization on Decision Making Personalization is one of the most powerful pillars of digital persuasion. Machine learning algorithms have the ability to shape our preferences and decisions, often without our full awareness. This chapter explores how personalization affects our decision making, and how the filter bubble can create an environment prone to confirming pre-existing beliefs, limiting the diversity of information and reinforcing specific behaviors.

Chapter 4: Persuasive Design and the Psychology of User Experience Digital interface design plays a crucial role in persuasion. UX (User Experience) and UI (User Interface) choices are made strategically to influence emotions and behaviors. In this chapter, we discuss how dark patterns, known as "dark patterns", are used to manipulate decisions, often to the detriment of users' interests. We also explore examples of persuasive design that maximizes engagement.

Chapter 5: The Psychology of Engagement and the Attention Economy The attention economy is a digital reality that reflects how companies compete for users' scarce attention. Dopamine, a neurotransmitter associated with pleasure, plays a central role here, being activated every time users receive rewards such as likes or notifications. This chapter explores the engagement mechanics of social media and other digital platforms, addressing how the positive feedback loop keeps users in a state of constant interaction.

Chapter 6: Persuasion and Decision Making in the Digital Environment Emotions and cognitive biases play a fundamental role in decision-making in the digital environment. Scarcity, urgency and fear are used strategically to induce specific behaviors, such as impulsive purchases or quick actions. We analyze how these factors influence the way we make decisions online, often without thinking deeply about the consequences.

Chapter 7: Neuromarketing and Subconscious Influence Neuromarketing explores how brain reactions can be predicted and influenced. Using technologies like eye tracking and electroencephalography (EEG), companies are able to understand how people react to certain stimuli and adapt their marketing strategies accordingly. This chapter discusses how visual stimuli, sound stimuli, and other factors can be manipulated to affect users' subconscious behavior.

Chapter 8: Artificial Intelligence and Algorithmic Persuasion Artificial intelligence has become one of the most powerful tools in digital persuasion. Through recommendation algorithms, AI is able to predict and influence behavior with impressive accuracy. In this chapter, we look at how AI is used to personalize offers, optimize the user experience, and even manipulate consumer choices. The ethics of using AI to persuade is also critically discussed.

Chapter 9: The Power of Stories and Persuasive Narrative Stories have immense power over how we understand the world and make decisions. This chapter explores how digital storytelling is used to create emotional connections and influence perceptions. Narrative psychology is applied in marketing and social media campaigns, where brands create engaging stories to increase consumer engagement and loyalty.

Chapter 10: Gamification and Reinforcement Psychology Gamification uses game elements to engage users, making interactions more engaging and motivating. Reinforcement psychology, which is based on rewards and punishments, is fundamental to understanding how digital platforms keep users active. This chapter explores how gamification can be applied in different contexts, such as education, healthcare and commerce, to improve engagement and achieve specific objectives.

Chapter 11: Social Media Persuasion: The Mass Effect Social media amplifies persuasion through social proof, that is, people's tendency to follow the actions and decisions of others. Digital influencers have the power to shape mass behavior, and content going viral can have a profound psychological impact. This chapter analyzes how social networks exploit the crowd effect to engage, influence and persuade users.

Chapter 12: The Effect of Colors, Sounds, and Shapes on Persuasion Visual and sound perceptions profoundly influence our emotions and decisions. Colors, sounds and shapes are used strategically in the design of digital platforms to generate specific emotional responses. This chapter explores how these elements are applied to increase the effectiveness of digital persuasion campaigns, based on case studies that demonstrate how design affects users' choices.

Chapter 13: Consumer Psychology and Online Shopper Behavior Digital consumer behavior is shaped by a range of psychological factors, including emotions, heuristics and mental triggers. This chapter discusses how companies use these factors to influence online purchasing decisions, creating an environment where consumers are encouraged to act quickly and often without thinking deeply about their choices.

Chapter 14: Persuasion and Fake News: How People Are Manipulated The spread of fake news is one of the most dangerous threats in the digital environment. This chapter looks at how algorithms amplify misinformation by taking advantage of people's confirmation biases and emotions. We explore the persuasive techniques used to create and spread false narratives, and how these narratives can influence public opinion and affect political and social decisions.

Chapter 15: Psychology of Fear and Urgency in the Digital Environment Fear and urgency are used strategically to generate immediate actions. Techniques such as scarcity and time pressure induce people to make quick, often impulsive decisions. This chapter examines how fear and urgency are applied in marketing and digital security, and the psychological impact of these strategies on users' decision-making.

Chapter 16: Persuasion in Digital Health and Wellbeing In this chapter, we discuss how digital persuasion is used in health and wellness apps to promote healthy behaviors. Persuasive technologies are designed to increase engagement and help users adopt healthy habits, but we also discuss the risks of digital overexposure and behavioral burnout.

Chapter 17: Digital Education and the Use of Persuasion for Engagement Modern educational platforms use persuasive techniques to increase student engagement and improve knowledge retention. This chapter explores how persuasion techniques are applied in the educational context, from gamification to content personalization, to optimize student learning and experience.

Chapter 18: Ethics and Transparency in the Psychology of Digital Persuasion Ethics in digital persuasion is a fundamental topic. In this chapter, we address the line between legitimate persuasion and manipulation, discussing the role of privacy, informed consent, and responsible practices in the use of digital psychology.

Chapter 19: How to Protect Yourself from Unwanted Persuasion The last chapter offers practical strategies for readers to protect themselves from unwanted persuasive techniques by increasing awareness of cognitive biases and digital traps. We present tools and practices to help users maintain their autonomy in online decisions and defend themselves from digital manipulation.

Chapter 20: The Future of Digital Persuasion In the last chapter, we address emerging technologies and new challenges in digital persuasion. The impact of new media and neural interfaces on human influence was discussed, as well as the need for a more conscious and ethical relationship with technology.

Final Reflection on the Psychology of Digital Persuasion

Understanding the psychology of digital persuasion is crucial for any individual navigating today's complex digital networks. As technologies continue to evolve, the influence over our decisions becomes increasingly sophisticated. Throughout this book, we have seen how different areas of psychology are applied in the digital world, from manipulating emotions and behaviors to using artificial intelligence and gamification to shape our actions.

The importance of understanding these techniques cannot be underestimated. In a world where purchasing decisions, political beliefs, opinions on health and well-being, and even everyday behaviors are increasingly influenced by digital platforms, being aware of the mechanisms of persuasion becomes a vital skill. Only in this way will we be able to maintain our autonomy and make conscious decisions, without being manipulated or exploited by the technologies that we depend on so much.

We would like to thank you, the reader, for engaging in this journey of reflection and learning. The digital world can be fascinating, but it is also a complex terrain where the lines between legitimate persuasion and manipulation can be blurred. We encourage you to continue reflecting on the topics covered and to apply this knowledge in a critical and responsible way. Technology is a powerful tool, but, like all tools, it depends on the conscious use we make of it.

Cordially,
Diego Rodrigues & Team!